M000307890

Life and Witness of Ezekiel

Life and Witness of Ezekiel

LARRY R. HELYER

CASCADE *Books* • Eugene, Oregon

LIFE AND WITNESS OF EZEKIEL

Cascade Books
An Imprint of Wipf and Stock Publishers
199 W. 8th Ave., Suite 3
Eugene, OR 97401

www.wipfandstock.com

PAPERBACK ISBN: 978-1-6667-1490-6
HARDCOVER ISBN: 978-1-6667-1491-3
EBOOK ISBN: 978-1-6667-1492-0

Cataloguing-in-Publication data:

Names: Helyer, Larry R. [author].

Title: The life and witness of Ezekiel / Larry R. Helyer

Description: Eugene, OR: Cascade Books, 2022 | Includes bibliographical references and index.

Identifiers: ISBN 978-1-6667-1490-6 (paperback) | ISBN 978-1-6667-1491-3 (hardcover) | ISBN 978-1-6667-1492-0 (ebook)

Subjects: LCSH: Bible.—Ezekiel—Criticism, interpretation, etc. | Bible.—Prophets—Criticism, interpretation, etc. | Prophets | Criticism, interpretation, etc.

Classification: BS1545.52 H45 2022 (paperback) | BS1545.52 (ebook)

VERSION NUMBER 082322

To the members of BASIC (Brothers and Sisters in Christ),
a small Bible study group at Providence Church
in Mount Juliet, Tennessee.

And in memory of Mike McKenzie, a member of our group
who is now with the Lord, "which is better by far" (Phil 1:23).

Contents

Preface

This book, like others in my Life and Witness series, had its genesis in the classroom. For nearly thirty years, I taught a class called "Hebrew Prophets" for undergrads at Taylor University. Because the course surveyed the entire corpus of OT literature designated as the "Prophetic Books" in the English Bible and "The Latter Prophets" in the Hebrew Bible, the luxury of an in-depth analysis of each individual prophetic work was simply not an option. While this was a limitation, it was also a benefit since it required selectivity in dealing with the specific contributions of each prophetic voice. The upshot is this book, a distillation of Ezekiel's enduring message for general readers.

I devote a disproportionate amount of attention to the first twelve chapters since this section lays out the primary issues and themes of Ezekiel's message. The rest of his prophecy, like a Mozart piano concerto, consists of variations on the principal motifs set out in the introductory chapters.

Special attention is paid to two features of prophetic activity requiring extended treatment. The first involves symbolic acts in which the medium is the message. As it turns out, Ezekiel is a master at street mime. No other Hebrew prophet engages in such elaborate and lengthy sign acts; indeed, he deserves an Oscar for his remarkable performance. His actions speak volumes without words! The cumulative impact on observers would be hard to overstate. The villagers of Tel Aviv (a camp for Jewish exiles in Babylon, modern Iraq) watched appalled and spellbound as

Yahweh's spokesperson shriveled up from starvation before their very eyes. Ezekiel's message was as clear as it was shocking: the inhabitants of Jerusalem would undergo similar starvation during an impending Babylonian siege. Added to this graphic portrayal was a little barbershop theology in which the prophet cut off his hair and sorted it into three piles corresponding to the differing fates of the Jerusalem citizens. There could be no doubt as to the tragic outcome of the siege.

A second noteworthy feature of Hebrew prophecy involved visionary experiences. In this regard Ezekiel is without peer. His visionary journey to Jerusalem is by far the most detailed account of Spirit levitation in sacred Scripture. What he saw and then related to his fellow exiles was as shocking as his starvation diet. He witnessed apostasy practiced by the most important leaders in the land, including the priesthood. Yahweh's verdict and sentence upon this wholesale defection was entirely appropriate and just.

Some readers may be disappointed in my treatment of Gog and Magog and the vision of a new temple. In my opinion, far too much energy has been expended trying to sort out end-times chronology and identify the protagonists rather than focusing on the theological message of the prophet. The same goes with the new temple, most often assigned to the millennial kingdom. The key here is reading the text in light of the fuller revelation of the NT. Read in canonical context, Ezekiel's vision of a new temple envisions ideal worship for a restored people in terms that made sense to a priest living under the old covenant. Now, under the new covenant, believers experience ideal worship when they "offer [their] bodies as a living sacrifice, holy and pleasing to God—this is [their] true and proper worship" (Rom 12:1; cf. John 4:23–24). This is so because believers, both individually and corporately, constitute the new temple of God (1 Cor 3:16; 6:19–20), "a dwelling in which God lives by his Spirit" (Eph 2:22) and in which they offer "spiritual sacrifices acceptable to God through Jesus Christ" (1 Pet 2:5).

Though I was aware that Ezekiel's thought leaves an imprint on the NT, the degree to which this is true was amplified after working through his prophecy, especially with the added insights of OT scholar Hassell Bullock. Accordingly, I have devoted an entire chapter setting out the links between Ezekiel and the NT, especially the ministry and teaching of Jesus of Nazareth.

May the book of Ezekiel be recovered in the preaching and teaching of churches and Christian institutions of higher education. The people of God across our planet find themselves increasingly living in troubling times, having much in common with the prophet Ezekiel and the Jewish exiles during the sixth century BC. In times like these, God's people need a fresh infusion of hope. Ezekiel's prophecy proclaims the most hopeful news the people of God could ever imagine: "For here we do not have an enduring city, but we are looking for the city that is to come" (Heb 13:14) because "The LORD is there" (Ezek 48:33). Like Abel of old, Ezekiel "still speaks, even though he is dead" (Heb 11:4). "Whoever has ears, let them hear what the Spirit says to the churches" (Rev 2:29; 2:11, 17, 29; 3:6, 13, 22).

Acknowledgements

Among those scholars seeking to provide a short, introductory-level study of Ezekiel, the book that caught my attention was H. L. Ellison's *Ezekiel: The Man and His Message*. In the compass of only 144 pages, Ellison expertly condenses the main features and themes of Ezekiel's prophecy. His work became a benchmark for my own endeavor.

For readers desiring to know who my primary conversation partners were in the writing of this book, the answer becomes apparent in footnotes. First among equals is the magisterial commentary by Daniel Block (*The Book of Ezekiel*, 2 vols). Another valued dialogue partner has been the eloquent and witty Christopher J. H. Wright (*The Message of Ezekiel*). His exposition is without peer in terms of readability and he accomplishes his task in 368 pages. The reader who seeks more depth than I can provide but isn't prepared to tackle Block (no pun intended!) is pointed to Wright's commentary. Many other scholars across a broad theological spectrum have illuminated my understanding of a complex and often opaque prophet. To them I owe a great deal indeed.

I do, however, want to give special recognition to Hassel Bullock. He wrote a paper entitled "Ezekiel, Bridge between the Testaments" published in *JETS* (1982) that expertly connects the dots between the ministry and thought of Ezekiel and Jesus. My gratefulness to him is readily apparent in chapter 10.

As always, I'm indebted to my most helpful editor and reader, my beloved wife Joyce. More times than I could possibly recount she has saved me from ambiguity, infelicity of expression, and that most pernicious affliction, scholarly obfuscation!

It's always a pleasure to work with the Cascade Books team. A special shout-out to my editor, Revd. Dr. Robin Parry, for a job well done. My roots run deep in the state of Oregon, especially the wheat fields of Sherman County. A person who has not witnessed a sunset behind Mount Hood from the east side of the Cascade mountains has missed a glorious sight!

List of Abbreviations

BIBLICAL TEXTS AND VERSIONS

ESV	English Standard Version
HCSB	Holman Christian Standard Bible
KJV	King James Version
LXX	Septuagint
MSG	*The Message: The Old Testament Prophets in Contemporary Language*
MT	Masoretic Text
NASB	New American Standard Bible
NET	New English Translation
NIV	New International Version
NJPS	Tanakh. The Holy Scripture: The New JPS Translation
NKJV	New King James Version
NRSV	New Revised Standard Version
NT	New Testament
OT	Old Testament
REB	Revised English Bible
TNIV	Today's New International Version

OTHER ANCIENT TEXTS

1QIsa^{a}	Cave One Qumran Isaiah manuscript copy a
ANET	*Ancient Near Eastern Texts Relating to the Old Testament*. 3rd ed., with suppl. Edited by J. B. Pritchard. Princeton: Princeton University Press, 1969.
Ant.	Josephus, *Antiquities of the Jews*
b.	Babylonian Talmud
B. Bat.	*Baba Batra*
Hist. eccl.	Eusebius, *Ecclesiastical History*
J. W.	Josephus, *Jewish War*
m.	Mishnah
OTP	*The Old Testament Pseudepigrapha*. Edited by James H. Charlesworth. 2 vols. Garden City, NY: Doubleday, 1983.
Sir	Sirach

SECONDARY SOURCES

AB	Anchor Bible
ABD	*The Anchor Bible Dictionary*. 6 vols. Edited by David Noel Freedman. New York: Doubleday, 1992.
BAR	*Biblical Archaeological Review*
BASOR	*Bulletin of the American Society of Oriental Studies*
BBC	Beacon Bible Commentary
BEB	*Baker Encyclopedia of the Bible*. 2 vols. Edited by Walter A. Elwell. Grand Rapids: Baker, 1988.
DCH	*The Dictionary of Classical Hebrew*. 8 vols. Edited by David J. A. Clines. Sheffield, UK: Sheffield Academic Press, 1993–2011.

EBC	Expositors Bible Commentary
IDB	*The Interpreter's Dictionary of the Bible.* 4 vols. Edited by G. A. Buttrick. Nashville: Abingdon, 1962.
IEJ	*Israel Exploration Journal*
ISBE	*International Standard Bible Encyclopedia.* 4 vols. Edited by G. Bromiley. Grand Rapids: Eerdmans, 1979–88.
JETS	*Journal of the Evangelical Theological Society*
JSOT	*Journal for the Study of the Old Testament*
JSOTSup	Journal for the Study of the Old Testament Supplement Series
NICOT	New International Commentary on the New Testament
NIDB	*New Interpreter's Dictionary of the Bible.* 5 vols. Edited by Katharine Doob Sakenfeld et al. Nashville: Abingdon, 2006–9.
NIVAC	New International Version Application Commentary
SRB	*The Scofield Reference Bible.* Edited by C. I. Scofield. New York: Oxford University Press, 1909.
TNIVSB	*The New International Version Study Bible.* Edited by Kenneth L. Barker et al. Grand Rapids: Zondervan, 2006.
TNTC	Tyndale New Testament Commentaries
TOTC	Tyndale Old Testament Commentaries
WJT	*Westminster Journal of Theology*
ZPEB	*Zondervan Pictorial Encyclopedia of the Bible.* 5 vols. Edited by Merrill C. Tenney. Grand Rapids: Zondervan, 1975.

1

Profile of a Prophet

This enigmatic person, easily the most bizarre of all the prophets.

—Christopher J. H. Wright

For most Bible readers Ezekiel is almost a closed book. Their knowledge of him extends little further than his mysterious vision of God's chariot-throne, with its wheels within wheels, and the vision of the valley of dry bones. Otherwise his book is as forbidding in its size as the prophet himself is in the complexity of his makeup.

—John B. Taylor

INTRODUCTION

Ezekiel marched to a different drum. Among the Hebrew prophets he stands out for his bizarre symbolic actions, his amazing visionary experiences, and his stoic attitude toward the rigors of the prophetic tasks assigned him.[1] Sometimes his behavior displays symptoms that modern psychologists and psychiatrists would classify as abnormal or, at the very least, dysfunctional.[2] For that reason, he exhibits a quite different psychological profile than his contemporaries. And yet, he shares a message very much in common with his distinguished predecessors, especially Jeremiah of Jerusalem, his contemporary. Both prophets, though over seven hundred travel miles apart, are on the same page theologically and hammer home the same themes. However, their styles and personalities couldn't be more divergent. Ezekiel occupies a unique niche in Yahweh's roster of prophets.

EZEKIEL'S BACKGROUND

So, who was this eccentric prophet whom Yahweh summoned into his service on July 31, 593 BC?[3] Born in 622 BC to Buzi, a member of a priestly family in the line of Zadok, Ezekiel's resume is disappointingly brief. Nothing further about Ezekiel's father, nor anything at all about his mother, childhood, or teenage years are known. Ezekiel's name means "may God strengthen," an appropriate name in light of the daunting task to which Yahweh summoned him. Like his contemporary Jeremiah, Ezekiel was divinely fortified to withstand the disappointment and discouragement of ministering to a rebellious and stubborn people without being afraid of them.[4]

We know he had a wife whom he dearly loved ("the delight of your eyes," Ezek 24:16), though she is never named and is

1. "For many Christians Ezekiel is too strange and his book too complex and bizarre to deserve serious attention" (Block, *Ezekiel*, 1:xi). Sweeney alerts readers: "He presents some of the most theologically challenging and dynamic material among the prophets of the Bible, and some of the most difficult and bizarre passages" ("Ezekiel," 1042).

2. "W. F. Albright described Ezekiel as one of the greatest spiritual figures of all time, in spite of his tendency to psychic abnormality—a tendency which he shares with many other spiritual leaders of mankind" (Boadt, "Ezekiel," 711).

3. For this precise dating, see Block, *Ezekiel*, 1:83.

4. Ezek 2:6–9; Jer 1:18–19.

mentioned only in an obituary notice synchronized with the fall of Jerusalem. No children are mentioned nor any reference to siblings or relatives.

According to a Jewish legend, Ezekiel was "buried at al-Kifl, near the modern town of Ḥillah in Iraq, not far from ancient Babylon.[5] It has been a Jewish shrine of some note."[6]

For a major prophet this is a meager personnel file indeed![7]

EZEKIEL THE EXILE

When we first meet Ezekiel in the book bearing his name, he is thirty years old[8] living in a settlement called Tel Aviv[9] along the Kebar River in ancient Babylonia (modern Iraq).[10] He is not living in Jerusalem because in 597 BC he had been deported along with King Jehoiachin, "the king's mother, his wives, his officials, and

5. Hillah was the scene of heavy fighting in the 2003 invasion of Iraq. Tragically, since its "pacification," a series of nine car bombs and suicide bombers have killed hundreds of Iraqis.

6. Boadt, "Ezekiel," 711.

7. There is more background information in Scripture for the two other major prophets, Isaiah and Jeremiah, especially the latter.

8. The NIV has "In my thirtieth year" (1:1). The Hebrew doesn't have the personal pronoun "my." NRSV, ESV, NKJV, and HCB simply read "In the thirtieth year." See discussion in Allen, *Ezekiel 1–19*, 20–21.

9. The first city founded by Jewish immigrants to Palestine in 1909 was named Tel Aviv. The name of the city means "Hill (or mound) of Spring." Today Tel Aviv is a bustling, modern city on the coast of Israel, the second largest city in the country after Jerusalem—with the reputation of a city that never sleeps—and the economic, industrial, and technological center of the country.

10. Though the Hebrew text uses the word *nahar* for the Kebar, technically, it was a canal, some sixty miles long, diverting water from the Euphrates River north of Babylon and then rejoining the Euphrates south of the city. The purpose of the canal was to irrigate fields along its course. Nebuchadnezzar probably relocated Judeans in this area to develop its potential and increase the food supply for the capital. This would be the first of many occasions when Jews were brought in to stimulate economic growth and oversee the production of goods. This role did not always prove beneficial for Jews because gentiles resented their oversight—especially in Poland and Russia during the eighteenth and nineteenth centuries.

the prominent people, . . . seven thousand fighting men, . . . and a thousand skilled workers and artisans" (2 Kgs 24:15–16). This was the punitive aftermath of Jehoiachin's futile rebellion against his overlord Nebuchadnezzar, king of Neo-Babylonia.[11]

The fact that Ezekiel was deported along with royal family members, army officers, and skilled workers distinguishes him from "the poorest people of the land" (2 Kgs 24:14). Furthermore, as a priest in training he possessed some valuable skills, especially the ability to read and write. That he was thirty years old when Yahweh called him is also significant—this was the age at which descendants of Aaron began active service in the temple.[12] Of course, being an exile far from home, Ezekiel had no realistic prospect of returning to Jerusalem and serving as a priest.

This reminds me of the character Hodel from the stage play and movie *Fiddler on the Roof*.[13] She falls in love with Perchik, a Jewish, political revolutionary, who is exiled to Siberia for his anti-Czarist views. Hodel chooses to marry Perchik (against her father Tevya's protestations) and join him in Siberia. In the poignant song "Far from the Home I Love" Hodel reflects back on the contentment and love she experienced in her family and in the little village of Anatevka. She ponders how a man unexpectedly changed her destiny. That's Ezekiel's story as well. The Neo-Babylonian King Nebuchadnezzar came on the scene and completely altered Ezekiel's future, forcing him to confront a new reality far from the home he loved.

Psalm 137 expresses what Ezekiel and many of his fellow Jews felt in their very bones: "By the rivers of Babylon we sat and wept when we remembered Zion. There on the poplars we hung our harps. . . . How can we sing the songs of the Lord while in a foreign land? If I forget you, Jerusalem, may my right hand forget its skill. May my tongue cling to the roof of my mouth if I do not remember you, if I do not consider Jerusalem my highest joy" (Ps 137:1–6).

11. 2 Kgs 24:10–17.

12. See Ellison, *Ezekiel*, 16–17.

13. The play is based on the book *Tevya's Daughters: Collected Stories of Sholem Aleichem*.

EZEKIEL THE PRIEST IN EXILE

Ezekiel's priestly background comes to expression throughout his book, especially in his vision of the restoration of the temple in the latter days and the reinstitution of the sacrificial rituals.[14] Though Isaiah and Jeremiah mention a future temple and sacrifices in passing, for Ezekiel this is a big deal. Ezekiel's climax of Israel's restoration features the restored priesthood offering "sacrifices of fat and blood" (Ezek 44:15), teaching the people "the difference between the holy and the common" and "how to distinguish between the unclean and the clean" (44:23). In fact, Ezekiel's interest in priestly ritual left an enduring legacy in postbiblical Judaism, so much so that some describe him as "the father of Judaism." Thus, even as a prophet, Ezekiel still functioned as a priest. The dual role of prophet and priest is another unique feature of Ezekiel's ministry.[15]

EZEKIEL THE JERUSALEMITE

Ezekiel grew up in Jerusalem and was familiar with the temple precincts. In fact, from his twentieth to his twenty-fifth year (when he was deported), he probably already served as an apprentice, learning the fine points of priestly ritual.[16]

He probably knew or was at least aware of Jeremiah the rogue prophet-priest from Anathoth who courageously announced the destruction of the temple in the days of Jehoiakim. Perhaps Ezekiel was even present on that dramatic day Jeremiah dropped a bombshell with his temple sermon delivered to a packed audience in the courtyard of the temple.[17] He may also have been in attendance four years later when Jeremiah's scroll was read out to

14. Besides Jeremiah, the prophet Zechariah was also a priest (Zech 1:1; cf. Neh 12:16). In the NT John the Baptist was the son of the priest Zechariah (Luke 1:5).

15. See also Petersen, "Introduction," 1222.

16. Ellison, *Ezekiel*, 17. See also Edersheim, *Temple*, 94–95.

17. Jer 7 and 26. See Helyer, *Jeremiah*, 19–38.

the assembled congregation for a specially called fast day.[18] Since Ezekiel's book strikes similar notes as Jeremiah, a linkage between these two sixth-century prophets necessarily enters into my exposition of the book of Ezekiel.[19]

Beyond this, we are limited to Ezekiel's prose and poetry for clues about his life and ministry in Tel Aviv. From these passages we glean a few more insights but I postpone further observations until we examine the texts.

EZEKIEL THE REFORMER

Using the Enneagram personality typing system, I think Ezekiel most closely resembles the Type 1 category, the reformer and perfectionist. Traits like being principled, self-controlled, and perfectionistic leap from the pages of his book. He possessed a strong sense of right and wrong, strove to improve things, was well-organized (see below under his literary skill) and fastidious. He struggled, however, with resentment and impatience because his fellow expatriate Jews did not share his intense commitment to the standard of holiness required by the Law of Moses.

Personality-wise, Ezekiel and Jeremiah are quite different. Ezekiel performs his prophetic task without protest (except for one minor instance). Jeremiah, however, has the chutzpah to push back and criticize Yahweh. For his part, Ezekiel carries out his calling as a compliant and uncomplaining watchman on the wall who never threatens to resign his prophetic calling like Jeremiah.[20]

18. Jer 36:9. Wright observes that "the event took place in 605 BC, when Ezekiel would have been about seventeen years old. He must have heard about it. It is very possible that he even witnessed the first reading of the scroll in the temple itself. Ezekiel's own recorded prophecies make it clear that he knew and made good use of the prophetic words of Jeremiah" (*Jeremiah*, 19). The reason for the specially called fast was probably owing to anxiety over Nebuchadnezzar's recent capture of Ashkelon on the Palestinian coast in December of 604 BC. In other words, the powerful Babylonian army was dangerously close and fear of an attack on Judah gripped the people.

19. See Wiersbe, *Be Reverent*, 241n2 for a list of relevant passages.

20. See Jer 20:9.

Ezekiel typically doesn't reveal his inner feelings—there are exceptions, such as after his initial call to be a prophet, when he informs the reader about the bitterness and anger in his spirit.[21] Jeremiah, of course, wears his feelings on his sleeves and makes no attempt to hide them from his readers; he even accuses Yahweh of deception and injustice in his famous complaints.[22] Ezekiel does, however, like Jeremiah, unleash judgment oracles upon his countrymen with deep-seated anger, reflecting the attitude of the Sovereign LORD who speaks through him.

Ezekiel's remarkable visionary visit to the Jerusalem temple in chapters 8–11 exposes apostasy and sacrilege. When the prophet recites a litany of covenant violations on the part of both priesthood and people, he includes a Levitical prohibition never mentioned by other prophets, namely, "to have sexual relations with a woman during her period" (Ezek 18:6).[23] His concern over strict adherence to ritual purity, a perfectionist trait, reflects his priestly training.

My purpose is not to prefer one prophet over the other but simply to appreciate a prominent feature of redemptive history. Yahweh calls very different types of people to serve as his spokespersons and each renders service in distinctive and sometimes idiosyncratic ways. The task before us in this book is to focus on Ezekiel's particular contribution to the message and theology of Scripture as stamped with his unique fingerprint.

EZEKIEL THE WRITER

While it is true Ezekiel's literary gifts are not as highly celebrated as the grand masters Isaiah and Jeremiah and his prose is "often ponderous and repetitive,"[24] he nonetheless deserves to sit at the same table with these giants. His poetic passages, though typically cast

21. Jer 3:14.

22. See Helyer, *Jeremiah*, 76–98.

23. See also Lev 18:19–20; 20:18.

24. Taylor, *Ezekiel*, 30.

in the form of somber funeral laments, can occasionally be vivid and intense. Though his metaphors occasionally contain sexually explicit and vulgar language, the emotional impact on the reader is palpable. This feature becomes another effective tool deployed by the prophet in order to grab the attention of an audience not inclined to accept his messages.

One facet of Ezekiel's writing sets him apart from his fellow prophets: he meticulously dates his oracles in chronological order. This is quite in contrast to Jeremiah's book in which the reader is toggled back and forth between early and late events often with no indication of date other than the context.

Thankfully, Ezekiel's book, in contrast to his complex personality, is straightforward and clearly organized—oh that the book of Jeremiah were so nicely laid out! In broad terms the book falls into five main sections:

I. Ezekiel's call and commission (Ezek 1–3)

II. Judgment oracles delivered prior to the fall of Jerusalem (Ezek 4–24)

III. Judgment oracles delivered against the nations (Ezek 25–32)

IV. Restoration oracles delivered after the fall of Jerusalem (Ezek 33–39)

V. Vision of a new temple and a restored priesthood (Ezek 40–48)

My task in the remaining chapters is to summarize and appreciate the prophet's message delivered in his inimitable preaching style.

2

Extraterrestrial Encounter at the Kebar

My son, we are pilgrims in an unholy land.

–*The Last Crusade*

It was Ezekiel who saw the vision of glory, which God showed him above the chariot of the cherubim.

—Sir 49:8

One may not expound upon the sexual rules (Lev 18, 20) in front of three [students], about creation (Gen 1) in front of two, or the chariot (Ezek 1) in front of (even) one, unless he is wise and already understands it on his own.

–*m. Ḥag.* 2:1

INTRODUCTION

The fifth day of the fourth month of the fifth year of King Jehoiachin's exile (July 31, 593/2 BC) was like none other for Ezekiel, featuring a spectacular pyrotechnic display that turned his world completely upside down. According to his account, he was "among the exiles by the Kebar River" (Ezek 1:1), when this shattering event took place.[1] It was nothing short of an opening of the heavens accompanied by a theophany, an appearance of the glory of Yahweh.

EZEKIEL'S INAUGURAL VISION (1:1–28)

Visionary experiences in connection with a prophetic call are not at all unusual, but Ezekiel's vision is off the charts![2] It begins from the outside, that is, with an approaching storm cloud "surrounded by brilliant light" (1:4), and moves inward to "the likeness of the glory of the LORD" (1:28) riding on his mobile throne-chariot above a crystal vault. Yahweh's throne-chariot is powered by four living creatures—later identified as cherubim—and surrounded by a brilliant, radiant light "like the appearance of a rainbow" (1:23). When the creatures moved the noise was deafening—"like the roar of rushing waters, like the voice of the Almighty, like the tumult of

1. Ezekiel's book is unique in that it is all written from a first-person perspective except for an editorial introduction to Ezekiel's call experience in 1:2–3. This fact has led most literary critics to acknowledge that the book is a unity. Jewish worshipers often met where there was running water for ritual purity reasons. When Paul visits Philippi on his second missionary journey, he and Silas go out to the Krenides River near the city of Philippi "where he expected to find a place of prayer" (Acts 16:13). He did find a small group of Jewish women, among whom was Lydia, the first convert in Europe (Acts 16:14).

2. "With respect to force and awesomeness, no theophany in the entire OT matches Ezekiel's inaugural vision, and modern readers can only regret that Ezekiel did not provide a visual image to accompany the text" (Block, *Ezekiel*, 1:106). For other examples see Isa 6:1–13; Jer 1:9–19.

an army" (1:24). To use a University of Oregon football analogy, it was like third down for a visiting team at Autzen Stadium![3]

Sinai Tabernacle

Ezekiel's depiction of Yahweh's throne-chariot differs from the Pentateuchal description of the Sinai tabernacle in that the latter begins with the innermost piece of furniture, the ark of the covenant, and proceeds outwards to the perimeter of the sacred enclosure, the courtyard curtains.[4]

In the tabernacle there is a notable absence: no image or representation of an animal, deity, or human being. The same is true of Ezekiel's vision of the throne-chariot, because the worship of Israel was aniconic, that is, without images representing the deity. Ezekiel's living creatures or cherubim are angelic beings not animals or humans and Ezekiel is careful to say that the figure on the throne was "*like* that of a man" (Ezek 1:26). The reason is profoundly simple: as soon as you select anything in the universe or the entire universe itself to represent God, you have already immeasurably reduced his being. Isaiah's rhetorical question is right on: "With whom, then, will you compare God? To what image will you liken him?" (Isa 40:18)—the expected answer is, no one and no thing in all creation.

3. In 2007 during a game between Oregon and USC, ESPN recorded a decibel level at 127.2. An Airbus 380 at takeoff reaches about 80 decibels. Here in middle Tennessee, we recently experienced an event that takes place every seventeen years, the reemergence of cicadas. The mating call of male cicadas can reach 100 decibels. Even the animal kingdom can't generate the noise level of Oregon football fans!

4. "There, above the cover between the two cherubim that are over the ark of the covenant law, I will meet with you and give you all my commands for the Israelites" (Exod 25:22). The narrative of setting up the tabernacle and its furniture also proceeds from the ark of the covenant outwards to the courtyard curtains (Exod 37–38).

Theological Significance

The order of description, whether one begins on the inside and works outward or vice versa, is not the important point. What is of supreme importance, however, is *Yahweh's awesome presence*—everything else is secondary. After the tabernacle with its tent of meeting and surrounding courtyard had been set up, "the cloud covered the tent of meeting and the glory of the Lord filled the tabernacle (Exod 40:14). Above the tabernacle at night, this cloud, blazing with fire, illuminated the way during nocturnal moves.[5] During the Mount Sinai theophany a thick cloud hung over the mountain and Yahweh descended in fire to the summit engulfed in billows of smoke, thunder peals, lightning, violent quaking, and a loud trumpet blast.[6]

The similarities between the Sinai ark of the covenant and the Kebar throne-chariot are striking, but so are the differences.[7] Most notably, the ark of the covenant had limited mobility—it must be transported from place to place on the shoulders of the Levitical Kohathites.[8] In contrast, Ezekiel's throne-chariot is highly mobile. Precisely this notion of omnipresent mobility revolutionizes Ezekiel's understanding of Yahweh's glory. In short, Ezekiel was not "beyond the pale."[9] Even in an unholy land the holy God

5. These nocturnal treks were probably undertaken to avoid the blistering heat of the Sinai desert during the day.

6. Exod 19:16–20.

7. The Hebrew term *merkavah* in reference to Yahweh's mobile throne-chariot is actually post-biblical (*m. Ḥag.* 4.1 [ca. 220 AD]). The word does, however, appear numerous times in the OT to refer to ordinary war chariots (e.g., Josh 11:6, 9; Judg 4:15; 1 Kgs 20:33, etc.). In modern Hebrew the term is used for Israel's most advanced battle tank—considered by many experts as one of the best in the world. In David's plan for the temple, the cherubim who overshadow the ark of the covenant are in fact equated with the "chariot" ([*merkavah*] 1 Chr 28:18). The cherubim in the Solomonic temple were huge—towering fifteen feet above the mercy seat (1 Kgs 6:23–26).

8. Num 4:15; 10:21; Deut 31:9; 2 Sam 6:13.

9. This expression refers to a boundary marking out an area or district. In Jewish history, during the Middle Ages and up until modern times, it referred to a region where Jews were permitted to live. They had to have permission to

was very much present. Armed with this new insight, he performs his calling as a watchman on the wall for the house of Israel as both a prophet who calls for repentance and a priest who calls for holiness.

Literary Significance

The inaugural vision reorients Ezekiel's view of reality and in so doing becomes the central organizing feature of his book. That is, the vision of Yahweh's glory frames his prophecies by employing an envelope or bookend arrangement.

Ezekiel's inaugural vision and his commissioning are followed by several chapters laying bare Jerusalem's blatant apostasy and announcing her imminent and just punishment by means of graphic and shocking symbolic actions.[10] In chapter 10 Ezekiel witnesses Yahweh's glory withdraw from the temple and depart toward the east (where Ezekiel was in exile!). The city's fate is sealed—city and temple will be consigned to the flames and its population either decimated or deported.

The bulk of the book unfolds in a series of judgment oracles against Israel and the surrounding pagan nations. A few salvation oracles, however, break through the gloom and offer a glimmer of hope for the future. Then, after a remarkable return to the land and a spiritual renewal, the united people of Israel undergo a massive invasion by an eschatological juggernaut symbolically named Gog and Magog.[11] Yahweh himself intervenes and rescues his people by utterly destroying the invader and his hordes. That leads to Ezekiel's lengthy, and perhaps tiring, description of a new eschatological temple far exceeding in scale and splendor anything ever seen before. The grand climax or bookend comes with the glory of Yahweh returning to a rebuilt and greatly expanded Jerusalem

---

leave this area. The point here is that Ezekiel thought he was beyond the region where God was present. How wrong he was!

10. Ezek 4–9.

11. Ezek 36–39.

temple resulting in a transformation of the Dead Sea area into a veritable garden of Eden.[12]

The Apostle John's Ascent to the Throne Room

I fast forward to the apostle John's description of the heavenly throne room in Rev 4. Raptured by the Spirit through an open door into heaven John sees "a throne with someone sitting on it" (Rev 4:2). Like Ezekiel's vision, John sees "a rainbow that shone like an emerald [and] encircled the throne" (Rev 4:3).[13] Arrayed around the throne were twenty-four elders, probably an angelic order, though some understand this group to represent the church. Closer to the throne are the seven spirits of God, perhaps the seven archangels.[14] Immediately surrounding the throne, four living creatures, similar to what Ezekiel saw, ceaselessly worship the Lord God Almighty rather than convey his throne-chariot.

John's masterful paradox in the dual image of "the Lion of the tribe of Judah, the root of David" juxtaposed with "a Lamb looking as if it had been slain" (Rev 5:5–6) initiates an outward movement from the throne to the perimeter of the cosmos.[15] Through a series of concentric circles beginning with the four living creatures and

12. Ezek 47:1–12.

13. Ezek 1:28. For the significance of the rainbow in redemptive history see Helyer, *Mountaintop*, 11–13.

14. Seven archangels are mentioned in Jewish traditions such as Tob 12:15; 1 En. 9:1; 54:6; and 2 En. 8:1–10:1. See Helyer, *Jewish Literature*, 69–71. Others suggest the sevenfold Holy Spirit of Isaiah based upon Isa 11:2.

15. John incorporates another profound paradox in his gospel. Enigmatic references to Jesus' hour or time when he will fully display his glory (John 2:4; 7:6; 8:20) finally arrives at the cross. From his cross, which serves as his throne, Jesus draws all people to [himself]" (John 12:23–33). In short, Jesus, innocent of the charges brought against him, seemingly died an unnecessary and unjust death. And yet, paradoxically, in his unjust death Christ justified the ungodly and triumphed over sin, death, and the demonic forces of evil headed up by the devil (2 Cor 5:18–21; Col 2:13–15; Heb 2:14–15). Perhaps the supreme irony of The Gospel of John is this: "the one who alone has the power to grant eternal life to men must himself die" (Barker et al., *New Testament Speaks*, 406).

twenty-four elders arrayed in close proximity to the throne, the camera, as it were, pulls back to reveal an encircling choir of the redeemed. Pulling back even farther, we now see a vast angelic choir "numbering thousands upon thousands" (Rev 5:11) encircling the throne room. Finally, arriving at the outer perimeter of the throne room, "every creature in heaven and on earth and under the earth and on the sea, and all that is in them" (Rev 5:13) comes into view.[16]

Try to imagine the throne-room scene as a cosmic concert. As one stands immediately before the throne, the cherubic quartet intones the words of the Trisagion: "Holy, holy, holy" (Rev 4:8)—this must have been loud because in Isaiah's vision of the throne room the seraphim voices were so loud "the doorposts and thresholds shook" (Isa 6:4). In John's vision, arrayed around the throne, the twenty-four elders chant a confession praising the God who "created all things" (Rev 4:11). After the Lamb takes the seven-sealed scroll, the decibel level increases significantly when the twenty-four elders join the four living creatures in singing a song of adoration to the Lamb who is "worthy to take the scroll" (Rev 4:9). As one moves further outward from the throne, the volume suddenly leaps off the decibel scale as the angelic hosts without number join in with another song of praise to the Lamb. Finally, on the perimeter, all creation pulsates with a mighty anthem "to him who sits on the throne and to the Lamb" (Rev 5:13)—an awe-inspiring scene, an acoustical and aesthetic tour de force, employing both visual and auditory imagery. The *Te Deum laudamus* gives voice to the moment: "all creation worships you."[17]

In short, John's Apocalypse incorporates both an inside out and an outside in method of description. In common with the description of the tabernacle and Ezekiel's throne-room vision,

16. The author of the *Temple Scroll* (one of the DSS found in cave 11 at Qumran) describes a gigantic new temple of the last days. He also begins with the innermost ring surrounding the holy of holies and proceeds outward so that the outermost ring encompasses the entire land of Israel (see Wise et al., *Dead Sea Scrolls*, 458, 470–78).

17. *The Book of Common Prayer*, 95. *The Song of the Three Young Jews* (Apocrypha) strikes the same note: "Bless the Lord, all you works of the Lord" (v. 35 [NRSV]; see the entire section vv. 29–65).

John's rapture to the throne room emphasizes a profound truth: God the Father and his Son Jesus Christ, the Lion and the Lamb, are the hub around which all things revolve. The apparent lack of mobility and movement for the throne in John's vision is more than counterbalanced by the fact that the entire universe revolves around it. Consequently, everything in the universe lies within the purview of the omnipotent, omnipresent, and omniscient God.

Theological Application

A brief word about cosmology and theology is in order. The ancient and medieval geocentric view of the cosmos eventually gave way to Copernicus' heliocentric model (the sun as the center) of emerging astronomy in the aftermath of the Enlightenment. The Bible simply reflects the ancient worldview ("It [the sun] rises at one end of the heavens and makes its circuit to the other . . ." [Ps 19:6]). Martin Luther scoffed at the view that the earth orbited the sun.

> There is talk of a new astrologer [Copernicus] who wants to prove that the earth moves and goes around instead of the sky, the sun, the moon, just as if somebody were moving in a carriage or ship might hold that he was sitting still and at rest while the earth and the trees walked and moved. But that is how things are nowadays: when a man wishes to be clever, he must . . . invent something special, and the way he does it must needs be the best! The fool wants to turn the whole art of astronomy upside-down. However, as Holy Scripture tells us, so did Joshua bid the sun to stand still and not the earth (Joshua 10:10–15).[18]

Luther lived before the recognition that the biblical account of creation was written from the standpoint of an observer relying only upon the naked eye. The theological teaching of Gen 1, however, is not invalidated by the discoveries of modern science. In fact, an astrophysicist may still speak of a beautiful sunrise or

18. Luther, *Luther's Works*, 358–59.

sunset even though she knows that is not a scientifically accurate description.

Modern astronomers have moved well beyond Copernicus and generally adhere to a big-bang cosmogony and an expanding-universe cosmology.[19] But in terms of ultimate reality, a more profound cosmological view is necessary, namely, a Christocentric worldview in which Jesus Christ is the center and focal point of the cosmos. "For in him all things have been created: things in heaven and on earth, visible and invisible, whether thrones or powers or rulers or authorities; all things have been created through him and for him . . . and in him all things hold together" (Col 2:16–17). Such a view, though empirically beyond proof, will never be replaced or updated—it is an eternal given. Whatever processes and developments have occurred or may be occurring in the vast reaches of space are all part of a master plan.

In the last episode of the original *Star Wars* trilogy, *The Return of the Jedi*, the evil Emperor Palpatine brings Luke Skywalker into his master control room in which monitors display what is happening in various parts of deep space. He points to a monitor showing that on the moon Endor Leia and Han have fallen into a trap and are about to be taken prisoner. With malignant satisfaction he tells Luke, "All is foreseen." How wrong he was! This cinematic creation is but a paltry imitation of a creator God who sovereignly rules his universe and is immediately and infallibly aware of all that transpires within it—as celebrated in the magnificent Ps 139. The believer may rest securely in this fact: "This is my Father's world." We all live and move within his twenty-four-seven surveillance camera.[20] We join the psalmist in exclaiming, "Such knowledge is too wonderful for me, too lofty for me to attain" (Ps 139:6).

It is also the key to living a life worthy of the Lamb who was slain. Christ at the center of one's life replicates a Christocentric

19. Cosmogony is the study of the origin of the universe and cosmology deals with the structure of the universe.

20. See also Acts 17:24–28

cosmos and is the secret of a fruitful and satisfying life.[21] Thus, the fulfillment of God's plan features "unity to all things in heaven and on earth under Christ" (Eph 1:10). This unity is certain because all things unfold "according to the plan of him who works out everything in conformity with the purpose of his will" (Eph 1:11). In short, "all is foreseen."

21. "At the center of the universe . . . there's a Creator with holes in his hands, drenching the cosmos in a gratuitous downpour of love. He doesn't have to—he just wants to. It's who he is. And when the lights go out, the real show begins" (Fischer, *Young, Restless*, 108).

EXCURSUS ON YAHWEH'S THRONE-CHARIOT AND THRONE

For those who would like to explore further the theme of Yahweh's throne-chariot I have appended the following background information. Otherwise, one may proceed directly to the next chapter, Ezekiel's commission as a watchman on the wall.

Other Sightings of the Throne-Chariot

The throne-chariot of Ezekiel's vision isn't unique in Scripture. There are other passages in which we catch a glimpse of this fascinating piece of divine conveyance.

Alien Space Craft

Before examining these, however, I first eliminate a much-ballyhooed explanation for Ezekiel's vision of the throne-chariot. According to this view, what really happened to Ezekiel was an extraterrestrial visit by a spacecraft belonging to an advanced civilization in deep space. Not a few enthusiasts of alien visitations from outer space have appealed to Ezekiel as evidence. Actually, a search for celestial life began in the early 1900s. One of the purposes of NASA, created in 1958, was to search for intelligent life on other planets, going under the acronym of SETI (search for extraterrestrial intelligence). Among its enthusiastic supporters have been the astrophysicist Stephen Hawking and Russian billionaire Yuri Milner.

When Erich von Däniken, a popularizer of the notion of visitors from outer space, published a book in 1968 entitled *Chariots of the Gods?* the idea of extraterrestrials gained considerable attention, reinforced by a steady diet of movies featuring extraterrestrial life, such as Steven Spielberg's 1982 blockbuster *ET*.[22] Although

22. Of course, many movies before *ET* featured visits or invasions by aliens, beginning as early as 1918 with *A Trip to Mars*. Clearly, Americans have been both fascinated and a bit worried about the possibility of extraterrestrial life.

von Däniken's book title concluded with a question mark, his presentation was more like advocacy than query. A prime witness for his thesis of course was Ezekiel's vision of the throne-chariot. I'll not spend time responding to von Däniken's arguments other than to say his book is a prime example of special pleading and woeful exegesis. For the reader who wishes to pursue in detail why von Däniken's thesis has no merit, I recommend *Crash Go the Chariots* by Clifford Wilson.

As to the larger question of intelligent life on other planets, so far, the verdict is negative. We appear to be an anomaly in a vast universe (or universes). This is not to say no intelligent life or even non-sentient life exists somewhere in the vast reaches of deep space. There may be. But as of right now, there is no evidence, only speculation.

Poetic Imagery

Several poetic texts in the Pentateuch, Psalter, and Prophets allude to Yahweh's chariot and mention the cherubim and clouds as accompanying accessories. "There is no one like the God of Jeshurun, who rides across the heavens to help you and on the clouds in his majesty" (Deut 33:26).[23] "He parted the heavens and came down; dark clouds were under his feet. He mounted the cherubim and flew; he soared on the wings of the wind. He made darkness his covering, his canopy around him—the dark rain clouds of the sky" (Ps 18:9–12). "He makes the clouds his chariot and rides on the wings of the wind" (Ps 104:3). "See, the LORD rides on a swift cloud and is coming to Egypt" (Isa 19:1).[24]

The Chariots and Horsemen of Israel

In addition to these poetic texts, we have the memorable story of Elijah's rapture to heaven. After Yahweh revealed to Elijah that his

23. Jeshurun is a poetic reference to Israel.

24. See also Job 38:1; Pss 68:4; 97:2–6; 104:3–4; Mic 1:3: Hab 3:8.

time on earth was up, he and his protégé Elisha cross the Jordan River and walk in the direction of Mount Nebo.[25] As they were talking together "suddenly a chariot of fire and horses of fire appeared and separated the two of them, and Elijah went up to heaven in a whirlwind. Elisha saw this and cried out 'My father! The chariots and horsemen of Israel!'" (2 Kgs 2:11–12). The chariots accompanying Elijah's rapture didn't actually snatch him up; he was transported in a whirlwind—contrary to the lyrics of the Black spiritual "Swing Low Sweet Chariot." But the chariots Elisha saw are linked in some way with Yahweh's throne-chariot. This becomes clearer when we turn to an incident during the ministry of Elisha ben Shaphat.

Chariots of Fire

Elisha's distraught response to the "chariots and horsemen of Israel" (2 Kgs 2:12) suggests that Yahweh is accompanied by an angelic entourage who also employ chariots for rapid transit. The notion of a multiplicity of heavenly chariots leads us to a fascinating episode in Elisha's ministry.

The setting is a war between Aram (modern Syria) and Israel (2 Kgs 6:8). Elisha routinely tips off the Israelite king about Aramean ambushes and troop movements. The infuriated Aramean monarch suspects a mole among his officers so he summons them to ferret out the informer. They loudly protest their innocence and point to the source of the leak: "Elisha the prophet who is in Israel, tells the king of Israel the very words you speak in your bedroom" (2 Kgs 6:12). Even pillow talk was on Elisha's prophetic wavelength!

Determined to regain the tactical advantage, the king of Aram decides to kidnap Elisha and turn the tables—Elisha's remarkable

25. The mention of Mount Nebo as the destination is fraught with theological significance because that is where Moses the great mediator of the Sinai covenant was buried by the LORD himself. Now as the champion and defender of the covenant finishes his prophetic ministry, he heads for the burial place of his illustrious predecessor, a fitting locale for his rapture. See Helyer, *Mountaintop*, 72–80.

clairvoyant capabilities will be enlisted to assist the Arameans. So, Elisha was tracked to the city of Dothan and a strong force deployed by night to surround the city with orders to capture the prophet alive. The historian narrates the ensuing story with a delightful sense of humor.

When Elisha's servant arose early the next morning, he saw the Aramean taskforce accompanied by a large chariot corps surrounding the city. He freaked out: "Oh no, my lord! What shall we do?" (2 Kgs 6:15). The thought of finishing his days as an Aramean slave completely unhinged him.

Elisha is as cool as a cucumber. Without bothering to explain the situation, he simply prays: "Open his eyes, Lord, so that he may see" (2 Kgs 6:17). Now it's not as if the servant's eyes were closed or full of eye sand! Elisha was referring to the invisible, spiritual realm, a dimension inaccessible to human observation unless granted divine permission. In this case, the servant was enabled to perceive what was there all along, just not visible to the naked eye.

Yahweh opened the servant's spiritual eyes and what a sight! The hills were "full of horses and chariots of fire all around Elisha" (2 Kgs 6:17).[26] Yahweh's personal chariot corps of angels was arrayed around the unsuspecting Aramean troops—they were the surrounded ones! To be sure, the angelic chariots are not on par with Yahweh's throne-chariot—that's an exclusive and restricted mode of divine transportation.

To sum up, Scripture does occasionally describe angelic beings who ride in chariots. The main idea, like that of Yahweh's throne-chariot, is mobility and power. These beings can intervene and provide divine assistance to God's saints. As Ps 68:17 indicates, they are a mighty host and thus available to God's people

26. I hear in my mind the theme song of the inspiring movie *Chariots of Fire*, the story of the 1922 Paris Olympics in which Eric Liddell, a devout Christian, won the 400 meters gold medal for Great Britain. After the Olympics, Eric served as a missionary in China. He died of a brain tumor in a Japanese concentration camp just before it was liberated by the Allies. His selfless service in the name of Christ was a powerful witness to his fellow prisoners.

wherever they may be: "The chariots of God are tens of thousands and thousands of thousands."[27]

Divine Throne Room

As it turns out, no other narrative passage depicts Yahweh's throne-chariot. But there are two OT passages that describe a heavenly throne room, to which I now turn.

Micaiah ben Imlah

The first occurrence is set in the ninth century BC when the notorious Ahab king of Israel entreated Jehoshaphat king of Judah to join him in an effort to drive the Arameans out of Ramoth Gilead. This city, which had been apportioned to the tribe of Gad in the days of Joshua, was an important check point along the King's Highway running from Damascus to the Gulf of Aqabah.[28] Whoever controlled this city collected tolls from caravans laden with valuable goods, a considerable income for the royal coffers.[29]

Jehoshaphat is reluctant to undertake the campaign without seeking divine guidance. "First seek the counsel of the LORD" (1 Kgs 22:5). Ahab obliges. He calls in his state-sponsored prophets—four hundred of them!—who allegedly speak in the name of Yahweh.[30] In reality, they are little more than propaganda agents

27. See also Isa 66:15; Zech 6:2–3.

28. Moses designated Ramoth Gilead as a city of refuge (Deut 4:43). During the apportionment of the land, Joshua assigned the city to the tribe of Gad (Josh 20:8; 21:38//1 Chr 6:80).

29. "N. Glueck . . . suggested Tell Ramith (M.R. 244210), 7 km S of Ramtha near the modern frontier with Syria (1943: 11–12), and this identification won scholarly approval in view of Ramith's etymological connections with Ramoth, its commanding location as a 'height' over the surrounding plain, and its Iron Age pottery" (Arnold, "Ramoth-Gilead," 5:620, citing Glueck, "Ramoth-Gilead," 11–12).

30. Recall that Elijah had earlier ordered the execution of 450 prophets of Baal (1 Kgs 18:40). Ahab's prophets in ch. 22 are not called prophets of Baal and are supposed to prophesy in the name of Yahweh (1 Kgs 22:6, 11).

for the king's agenda. Not surprisingly, they unanimously and vociferously tell the king exactly what he wants to hear: "Go," they answered, "for the LORD will give it into the king's hand" (1 Kgs 22:6).

Jehoshaphat is no dummy. He is quite aware that Ahab's prophets are on the payroll and prophesy in accord with the desires and interests of the crown. He requests that a prophet of Yahweh be consulted—a not-so-subtle dismissal of Ahab's so-called prophets of Yahweh!

Ahab concedes that there is one prophet who could inquire of Yahweh, but he hates him "because he never prophecies anything good about me, but always bad" (1 Kgs 22:8). Jehoshaphat wants to hear from him and Ahab reluctantly summons Micaiah ben Imlah, a prophet about whom we know nothing else other than what is recorded in this narrative.

Micaiah adopts an interesting strategy.[31] Although warned ahead of time about the unanimous prediction of success, Micaiah courageously commits to telling the two kings only what Yahweh reveals.[32] At first, however, he appears to chime in with Ahab's prophets. The reader must read between the lines and try to imagine Micaiah's manner and tone of delivery. Obviously, he delivered his prophetic exhortation in a mocking, sarcastic tone because Ahab immediately protested: "How many times must I make you swear to tell me nothing but the truth in the name of the LORD?" (1 Kgs 22:16).

At this point, Micaiah drops all pretense and describes a vision. The imagery of scattered sheep with no shepherd would have instantly been understood as a prediction of Ahab's death and the defeat of his army.[33] Ahab vents his frustration with Micaiah:

31. In this he reminds us of Jeremiah who appeared to agree with the false prophet Hananiah (Jer 28:5–8) before lowering the boom on him later (Jer 28:15–17).

32. 1 Kgs 22:13–14.

33. This draws on the widespread metaphor of Middle Eastern kings as shepherds. See Psa 78:70–72 and Helyer, *Life and Witness of David*, 52–53.

"Didn't I tell you that he never prophesied anything good about me, but only bad?" (1 Kgs 22:18).

Micaiah doesn't stop there. He proceeds to describe his vision in more detail—a fascinating portrayal of the heavenly throne room. Micaiah not only saw the throne; he also overheard the heavenly deliberations going on with "the multitudes of heaven" arrayed around Yahweh (1 Kgs 22:19).

Yahweh calls for a volunteer from his angelic court attendants, "Who will entice Ahab into attacking Ramoth Gilead and going to his death there?" (2 Kgs 22:19). A spirit steps forward and agrees to go forth and deceive Ahab's state prophets into urging the king to attack with the promise of complete success. Micaiah breaks off his description with a judgment oracle: "The LORD has decreed disaster for you [i.e., the king]" (1 Kgs 22:23).

Micaiah's odd-man-out prediction doesn't go unchallenged. Zedekiah ben Kenaanah slaps Micaiah in the face and taunts him. The infuriated King Ahab consigns Micaiah to prison on a bread and water ration until he returns safely.[34] As he was being taken away, Micaiah reminds the assembled war council of a fundamental test of true prophecy, namely, whatever is spoken in the name of the LORD will take place; otherwise, it's a false prophecy.[35] In the end, Micaiah was proven to be a true prophet of Yahweh because Ahab did not return in safety; he died on the battlefield.[36]

Isaiah ben Amoz

Our second heavenly throne-room vision occurred about a century later. After a relatively peaceful and prosperous reign of fifty-two-years, King Uzziah of Judah died (ca. 740 BC). Unfortunately, ominous signs that portended difficult days ahead appeared on

34. 1 Kgs 22:24. For a parallel in the life of Jeremiah who was likewise challenged by a false prophet and imprisoned see Jer 28; 37–38 and Helyer, *Jeremiah*, 13–15.

35. Deut 18:21–22. See Helyer, *Yesterday*, 281.

36. 1 Kgs 22:29–38.

the horizon.[37] That very year Yahweh summoned Isaiah ben Amoz into his heavenly council chamber and charged him with a daunting mission.

Isaiah is justly called the "prince of the prophets." His literary and rhetorical skills are without peer; his theological grasp of redemptive history and the scope of his proclamation, unrivaled; his portraits of the coming Messiah, the most breathtaking and complete, earning him the accolade "the evangelical prophet." The fourth of the so-called "Servant Songs" (Isa 52:12—53:13) ascends to what I consider the Mount Everest of OT theology—the doctrine of vicarious, substitutionary atonement accomplished by the Servant of Yahweh.[38]

In his call vision Isaiah saw Yahweh's awesome throne room. His attention was immediately focused on Yahweh sitting on his throne "high and exalted" (Isa 6:1). Especially striking was his magnificent robe with a long train filling the heavenly temple. Images of the beautiful trains trailing behind Princesses Diana and Kate during their bridal processions down the long central aisle of venerable Westminster Cathedral in London come to mind.

Flying above Yahweh were seraphim, perhaps synonymous with the four living creatures or cherubim described by Ezekiel. There are, however, several differences. Ezekiel's cherubim apparently have only four wings whereas Isaiah says the seraphim have six. "With two wings they covered their faces, with two they covered their feet, and with two they were flying" (Isa 6:2). Moreover, their relative positions vis-á-vis the throne and their functions differ. Whereas the cherubim power Yahweh's mobile throne-chariot from below, Isaiah's seraphim fly above it like angelic escorts. In light of this, we should probably distinguish between these two angelic orders.[39]

37. "By the end of his reign, however, clouds were gathering: Tiglath-Pileser III of Assyria, who acceded in 745 BC, was an imperialist, and already the small Palestinian states were feeling the threat. It is tempting to think of Isaiah, pondering the old king's death, anxious for the future, being comforted by the vision of a King who cannot die (cf. *the King*, 5)." (Motyer, *Isaiah*, 79).

38. See Helyer, *Yesterday*, 256.

39. See Elwell, "Seraph, Seraphim," 2:1926–27 and Smith, "Seraphim," 4:410–11.

Isaiah's throne-room theophany completely undid him. "I am ruined! For I am a man of unclean lips, and I live among a people of unclean lips, and I have seen the King, the LORD almighty" (Isa 6:5). But as always, Yahweh's summons to service is accompanied by sustaining grace. In a visionary and symbolic action, one of the seraphim touched his lips with a live coal and uttered this word of absolution: "See, this has touched your lips; your guilt is taken away and your sins atoned for" (Isa 6:7). What a turnaround in Isaiah's attitude: "Here am I, send me!" (v. 8).

Liturgical References to Yahweh's Throne

First Kings 22 and Isaiah 6 are the only OT visionary descriptions of Yahweh's throne room placed in a narrative setting. But as already mentioned in the introduction, several poetic passages in the Psalms make reference to the heavenly throne. I select several to illustrate how the imagery of Yahweh's throne functions in Hebrew liturgy:[40]

"The LORD reigns forever; he has established his throne for judgment. He rules the world in righteousness and judges the people with equity" (Ps 9:7).

"The LORD is in his holy temple; the LORD is on his holy throne. He observes everyone on earth; his eyes examine them" (Ps 11:4).

"Your throne, O God, will last for ever and ever; a scepter of justice will be the scepter of your kingdom" (Ps 45:6).

"Clouds and thick darkness surround him; righteousness and justice are the foundation of his throne" (Ps 97:2).

"The LORD has established his throne in heaven, and his kingdom rules over all" (Ps 103:19).

"Hear us Shepherd of Israel, you who lead Joseph like a flock. You who sit enthroned between the cherubim" (Ps 80:1).

40. The Psalm references, however, are to the ark of the covenant guarded by the cherubim in either the heavenly temple or its earthly counterpart in the Jerusalem temple and not the mobile throne-chariot of Ezekiel's vision.

"The Lord reigns, let the nations tremble; he sits enthroned between the cherubim, let the earth shake. Great is the Lord in Zion; he is exalted over all nations" (Ps 99:1).

Synthesizing the foregoing texts yields the following theological truths:

- Yahweh is the eternal and holy God
- He is the sovereign God who reigns and rules over all his creation
- He is the supreme, just, and righteous judge who requires justice and righteousness of all peoples
- Israel enjoys a special relationship with Yahweh

These fundamental theological affirmations are implicit in Ezekiel's vision of the glory of Yahweh and his dazzling throne-chariot on the banks of the Kebar. Ezekiel's prophetic call, however, to be a watchman puts special emphasis on the fourth affirmation, Israel's role in Yahweh's economy. In fact, this unique relationship is the primary focus of Ezekiel's ministry.

Throne-Room Theology and Typology

Throne-room imagery also functions at the canonical level and ties the testaments together by means of typology. Thus, Moses was instructed to "make this tabernacle and all its furnishings exactly like the pattern I will show you" (Exod 25:9). According to 1 Chr 28:19–20, Yahweh gave David detailed plans for the construction of the Jerusalem temple. Solomon was warned that he "must see that everything is done according to these plans." Both tabernacle and temple were copies of a heavenly archetype—Yahweh's heavenly temple and throne room. That is a major point of emphasis picked up by the writer of Hebrews. He argues that Christ poured out his sacrificial blood for sinners in the true, heavenly sanctuary not a mere copy or shadow.[41] Furthermore, the heavenly temple

41. Heb 9:11–13, 24.

and throne room play a major role in the message of the book of Revelation.[42] From his throne the Lord rules over all things and accomplishes his purpose for all creation.

Metaphor and Reality

The reader has probably entertained an important question. Are the throne-chariot and the throne of God real? Should these passages be interpreted literally or metaphorically?

In my view, they are metaphorical. A throne or throne-chariot represents a fundamental theological truth, namely, the rule and sovereignty of God. The ancient Near East provides numerous illustrations of literal thrones and cherubim who guard thrones. These were real artifacts depicted on wall reliefs from the palaces of Assyrian, Babylonian, and Persian kings. Solomon also had a magnificent throne of ivory overlaid with gold and flanked by two lion figures beside the armrests: The narrator notes that "nothing like it had ever been made for any other kingdom" (1 Kgs 10:20; see vv. 18–19).

But Ezekiel's throne-chariot is something he saw in "visions of God" (Ezek 1:1). The same is true of Isaiah ben Amoz and Micaiah ben Imlah's vision of Yahweh's throne room. Typically, prophetic visionary accounts combine both the real and the imaginary. For example, the throne-chariot vision employs imagery drawn from the real world, such as a storm cloud and a chariot with wheels. But the depiction of the chariot and its accompanying phenomena spills over into the world of the fantastic.

Leland Ryken reminds us, "Our first task [as interpreters] is to open ourselves to the wonder, mystery, and otherness of the venture. For people who have antennae only for literary realism . . . parts of the Bible will remain a closed book."[43] Robert Traina insists that "literal and figurative approaches are not necessarily concerned respectively with fact and fiction. For they are simply

42. See Rev 4–5; 7:9, 11, 15; 8:3; 12:51; 14:3; 16:17; 19:4–5; 21:3, 5; 22:1, 3.

43. Ryken, *Reading the Bible*, 77.

two forms of literary expression; and an event which has actually occurred may be communicated by an author by either means."[44] Recognizing that Scripture employs figurative (metaphorical) language to communicate its message enables the reader to appreciate the nuances and rich texture of divine revelation. In short, the point made by the throne metaphor is real and celebrated in the book of Psalms: "The Lord reigns" (Ps 47:8; See also Pss 93:1; 96:10; 97:1; 99:1). Redemptive history concludes with a deafening shout: "Hallelujah! For our Lord God Almighty reigns. Let us rejoice and be glad and give him glory!" (Rev 19:6–7).

Human Reactions to Theophanies

Before leaving this topic, I draw attention to Ezekiel's reaction to the Kebar theophany: "When I saw it, I fell facedown" (Ezek 1:28). Encountering the divine presence produces an inevitable response—primal fear. Such an instinctive reaction stems from the immense gap a finite, sinful, temporal being senses in the presence of an infinite, holy, self-existent being. For mere mortals, to encounter the numinous (the supernatural) is to court destruction.

One recalls Jacob's dream at Bethel, a stairway reaching to heaven with Yahweh standing above it and reiterating the Abrahamic promise. Upon awakening, Jacob's reaction bordered on panic. "'Surely the Lord is in this place, and I was not aware of it.' He was afraid and said 'How awesome is this place!'" (Gen 28:16–17).

Moses's response to Yahweh's voice at the burning bush followed suit: "Moses hid his face, because he was afraid to look at God" (Exod 3:6). Later Moses requested to see God's glory. Yahweh consented with an important qualification: "You cannot see my face, for no one may see me and live" (Exod 33:20). So Yahweh placed Moses in the cleft of a rock, covered him with his hand until he had passed by, and then removed his hand allowing Moses to see his back.

44. Traina, *Methodical*, 175–76.

When "the commander of the army of the LORD" (Josh 6:14) appeared to Joshua near Jericho, he "fell facedown to the ground in reverence" (v. 14).[45] In the days of the judges, Manoah and his wife were personally visited by the angel of Yahweh to announce the coming birth of their son Samson. At first, they didn't realize it was Yahweh; they thought he was "a man of God [i.e., a prophet] . . . [who] looked like an angel of God" (Judg 13:6). But when Manoah realized that it was actually Yahweh himself who visited them, he was terrified: "'We are doomed to die!' he said to his wife. 'We have seen God!'" (Judg 13:21–22).

After being threatened by Jezebel, the dejected Elijah fled to Horeb (Mount Sinai). There Yahweh summoned him to "stand on the mountain in the presence of the LORD for the LORD is about to pass by" (1 Kgs 19:11). Going before Yahweh was a powerful wind, an earthquake, and a fire. Then "came a gentle whisper." (v. 12). Elijah knew it was Yahweh. "When he heard it, he pulled his cloak over his face and went out and stood at the mouth of the cave" (v. 13). He dared not look at Yahweh.

We've already discussed Isaiah's distraught reaction to his vision of Yahweh seated on his throne in the heavenly temple.[46]

In the era of the new covenant, the same human reaction to a theophany invariably occurs. Once during Jesus' ministry, a furious squall on the lake of Galilee suddenly swept over the disciple's boat. Fearing for their lives, they frantically awakened Jesus who was asleep in the stern. He simply commanded the waves, "Quiet! Be still!" (Mark 4:39; cf. Matt 8:23–27; Luke 8:22–25). Their reaction was predictable. "They were terrified and asked each other, 'Who is this? Even the wind and the waves obey him!'" (Mark

45. Note that Joshua was commanded: "take off your sandals, for the place where you are standing is holy" (Josh 5:15). That is precisely what Moses was instructed to do at the burning bush (Exod 3:5) and it was clearly Yahweh who was calling to him (Exod 3:6).

46. In the Apocryphal book Prayer of Manasseh, the repentant king expresses the universal reaction of mere mortals in the presence of the Almighty "at whom all things shudder, and tremble before [his] power, for [his] glorious splendor cannot be borne" (Pr Man 4–5). For the biblical account of Manasseh see 2 Chr 33:1–20. Pr Man is generally dated to the second or first century BC.

4:41). In an episode reminding us of Moses' encounter with God on Mount Sinai, Peter, James, and John witnessed Jesus' transfiguration on a mountain in Galilee. When Jesus' divine nature was unveiled in dazzling light and God's voice sounded forth from the bright cloud, "they fell facedown to the ground, terrified" (Matt 17:6). On his way to Damascus, Saul of Tarsus encountered the risen Christ and "suddenly a light from heaven flashed around him" (Acts 9:3). His reaction: "He fell to the ground" (v. 4). The apostle John's vision of the risen Christ on the island of Patmos produced a similar reaction. "When I saw him, I fell at his feet as though dead. Then he placed his right hand on me and said: 'Do not be afraid'" (Rev 1:17).

Personal Application

These inspired records of human responses to theophanies convey a salutary reminder—God is truly awe-inspiring and beyond all human comprehension.[47] An immense ontological gap separates him from us, mere mortals, and chastens our cavalier notions of autonomy and invincibility.[48] The appropriate responses to the being and character of God ought to be reverence, obedience, and worship. God's grace and mercy are likewise beyond all human reckoning. Contrition and confession are prerequisites to come boldly into his presence and lift our petitions and praises.[49] Recognizing "I need thee every hour" rebukes my tendency to call upon him only during times of crisis and distress. Nor should I be chummy with God and treat him as a good buddy—a cheeky attitude having no place in the life of a believer. Like the heroes of

47. The word "awesome" is one of the most misused and overused words in colloquial English. But when referring to God it is always appropriate.

48. Ontology has to do with the nature of being and existence. God is the self-existent one; we are created beings. Our minds simply can't comprehend or explain a being who always was, is, and will be. Like people stuck in a matrix we can't get outside our box. And so it shall always be, even when we are glorified.

49. Heb 10:19–23.

faith who preceded us, a facedown attitude before God is the prelude to divine blessing: As the inspired sage says, "The fear of the LORD is the beginning of knowledge" (Prov 1:7). More than ever, our generation needs to recover the biblical sense of reverence.[50]

50. "One thing that is lacking in the church today is a sincere reverence for the name and glory of the Lord" (Wiersbe, *Ezekiel*, 7). "The book of Ezekiel can help me, because reverence is the Big Idea that runs throughout this book" (Wiersbe, *Be Reverent*, 6).

3

Ezekiel's Call and Commission

Bound and gagged, hog-tied and tongue-tied—what possible way was that to be a prophet?

—Christopher J. H. Wright

EZEKIEL'S CALL (2:1—3:27)

In chapters 2 and 3 Ezekiel narrates his call and commission to be a prophet of Yahweh. This process involved several distinct phases, each of which throws light on the prophetic role. On any reckoning, functioning as Yahweh's messenger is an intimidating prospect and Scripture records that many who were called to the office initially begged off. One recalls the pleas to opt out by Moses, Jeremiah, and that most reluctant of prophets, Jonah ben Amittai. To his credit Ezekiel doesn't protest, although some suggest that the reference to his being "in bitterness and in anger" (3:15) implies his inner resistance to wearing the prophetic mantle.[1] Perhaps, but

1. "It must have been as unwelcome to Ezekiel as it was to Moses and

I think his indignation was directed at his fellow expatriates because of their hardness of heart and stubbornness.[2]

Enabling of the Spirit

Ezekiel's task will not be easy. When one surveys the "goodly fellowship of the prophets," all faced daunting circumstances.[3] None were able, apart from the Spirit's enabling, to carry out their mission. Ezekiel's call and commission takes us through a series of initiatory rites, each of which was foundational and transformational for his ministry.

Of first importance is the notice that "the Spirit came into me and raised me to my feet" (2:2). The post-exilic prophet Zechariah sums it up best: "Not by might nor by power, but by my Spirit, says the LORD Almighty" (Zech 4:6). In both Testaments the Spirit functions as the "energizer bunny" who enables Yahweh's servants to carry out their mission.

The infilling of the Spirit enabled Ezekiel to accomplish two things. First, it helped him to prove to his audience "that a prophet has been among them" (2:5). This was finally acknowledged by the Judean exiles after Ezekiel's elaborate and shocking symbolic

---

Jeremiah before him, though, unlike the call narrative of those two illustrious predecessors, there is no record of any words of protest from Ezekiel himself—although 3:14 hints that there was no shortage of such sentiment in his mind" (Wright, *Ezekiel*, 57). Block agrees: "Thus he sat among his fellow exiles for an entire week, resisting the call of God, but feeling the relentless pressure of God's hand" (*Ezekiel*, 1:138).

2. Ezekiel expresses the same outrage as the anonymous psalmist: "Indignation grips me because of the wicked, who have forsaken your law" (Ps 119:53; cf. 119:139). Jeremiah was also deeply distressed by the blatant apostasy of his fellow Judeans (Jer 15:17; 4:19; 23:9) and Ezra the priest was appalled by the intermarriage of Judeans with neighboring peoples (Ezra 9:3). John the Baptist had harsh words for the self-righteous Pharisees and complacent Sadducees: "You brood of vipers! Who warned you to flee the coming wrath! (Matt 3:7; Luke 3:7). The Master really unloaded on the hypocritical teachers of the law and the Pharisees (see Matt 23) using similar language as John.

3. The felicitous description of the prophets is from *Te Deum laudamus* (*Common Prayer*, 95).

actions depicting the fall of Jerusalem came to pass.[4] Secondly, the Spirit enabled the prophet to persist in the face of rejection and threats. Ezekiel was as "unyielding and hardened" in proclaiming his unpopular message as his listeners were in resisting it. "I will make your forehead like the hardest stone, harder than flint" (2:9). One is reminded of the Servant of the Lord in Isa 50:7: "Therefore have I set my face like flint, and I know I will not be put to shame." Luke alludes to this passage when he describes Jesus' attitude as he approached Jerusalem for the last time: "he set his face to go to Jerusalem" (Luke 9:51 NRSV). Yahweh told Jeremiah "Do not be afraid of them, for I am with you and will rescue you" (Jer 1:8). And he exhorted Ezekiel, "Do not be afraid of them or their words" (Ezek 2:6). There is no indication fear ever paralyzed either prophet in the performance of their duty, even though several times Jeremiah faced the very real prospect of death.[5]

Ingestion of the Word

The second phase involved a visionary experience of great importance. "I saw a hand stretched out to me" (2:9). In Yahweh's extended hand was an unrolled scroll so full it was written on front and back. The content was ominous: "words of lament and mourning and woe" (2:9). Like the other two major prophets, Isaiah and Jeremiah, the bulk of Ezekiel's prophecies are judgment oracles directed against Israel and Judah, and like the immense storm cloud of his inaugural vision, they darken the pages of his scroll. Thankfully, every now and then, a glimmer of sunlight breaks through the darkness and Yahweh's glory brightens the landscape, or, to borrow the imagery of C. S. Lewis, springtime returns to Narnia.

Ezekiel "must speak [Yahweh's] word to them" (2:7). That's the primary point of the vision of the scroll and the essence of what it means to be a prophet of Yahweh. Ezekiel doesn't simply take the scroll, he is commanded to eat it, which he does. The idea

4. Ezek 14:26–27; 33:23–33.

5. See Jer 26:11, 14–15; 37:20. Jeremiah's courage in the face of life-threatening situations was extraordinary. See Helyer, *Jeremiah*, 27–29.

seems to be that the prophet so assimilates God's word it becomes the marrow of his messages.[6]

Are we to suppose that the book of Ezekiel is identical with the contents of the scroll? Or is the vision symbolic of what Ezekiel himself would write guided by the Spirit? The evidence favors the latter alternative. Ezekiel's own personality and perspectives shine forth from the pages of his book. To think that the prophet simply copied a written text goes against the abundant evidence that in Scripture God speaks through authentic human voices. Luther was fond of the analogy of swaddling clothes. Just as the babe Jesus, the incarnate Word of God, was wrapped in swaddling clothes (i.e., genuine humanity), so too is the written word of God. It is the Spirit who superintends this mysterious process whereby the finished product, while a human text, is "God-breathed and is useful for teaching, rebuking, correcting and training in righteousness, so that the servant of God may be thoroughly equipped for every good work" (2 Tim 3:16–17).

Ezekiel's reception of the God-breathed word was a pleasant experience: "sweet as honey in my mouth" (Ezek 3:3). Jeremiah felt the same way: "When your words came, I ate them; they were my joy and my heart's delight" (Jer 15:16). A Psalmist concurs: "How sweet are your words to my taste, sweeter than honey to my mouth" (Ps 119:103). Pastor John of Patmos also enjoyed the taste of the word, but the digestion process proved to be quite unpleasant: "my stomach turned sour" (Rev 10:10).[7] Jeremiah and Ezekiel suffered similar gastrointestinal problems. The burden of proclaiming Yahweh's judgment, especially upon one's own people, exacts a heavy toll. Jeremiah speaks for his fellow prophets: "Oh, my anguish, my anguish! I writhe in pain. Oh, the agony of my heart! My heart pounds within me, I cannot keep silent" (Jer 4:19).

6. "Merely hearing that message is obviously not enough: it must be digested, internalized, incorporated, embodied, and lived. The medium becomes the message" (Block, *Ezekiel*, 1:131).

7. Pastor John was Eugene Peterson's favorite designation for John in the book of Revelation (*Pastor*, 237).

COMMISSION AS A WATCHMAN (3:16–21)

Seven silent, distressing days among the refugees at Tel Aviv elapse. On the eighth day another word from Yahweh breaks the silence.

Background of Ezekiel's Commission

Before going into specifics, I need to explain the unspoken but essential background of Ezekiel's commission. This passage presupposes a unique relationship between Yahweh and his people Israel: "For you are a people holy to the LORD your God. The LORD your God has chosen you out of all the peoples on the face of the earth to be his people, his treasured possession" (Deut 7:6). The stipulations of Israel's covenant with Yahweh are spelled out in the Sinai covenant and require complete loyalty and obedience.[8] But therein lay the problem: "Son of man, I am sending you to . . . a rebellious nation that has rebelled against me; they and their ancestors have been in revolt against me to this very day" (Ezek 2:3). As a result, the ultimate sanction for covenant violations, namely, expulsion from the land, was in the process of being carried out.[9]

That's the bad news. The good news is that Yahweh isn't finished with Israel yet. This is demonstrated by his glorious presence in a land of spiritual darkness and moral depravity. The way home lies in repentance and reform. Ezekiel's task, like that of his contemporary Jeremiah, is to call the faithless people of God back to covenant faithfulness. To accomplish this task the faithful God of faithless Israel calls Ezekiel to be a faithful watchman on the wall.

Meaning of the Metaphor

The modern reader of this text probably has some idea what a watchman did in biblical times, but a bit of background throws more light on this responsibility. Posting watchmen on city walls,

8. See further Helyer, *Yesterday*, 138–48.

9. See Lev 26:33–35; Deut 28:64–68.

in towers and turrets placed at intervals along the course of the wall, was primarily for security purposes. Watchmen were charged with reporting any sign of hostile military action against the city or civil unrest within.[10] Watchmen also signaled the dawn of a new day, probably with trumpet blasts.[11]

As watchmen, prophets were privy to Yahweh's determination to punish the nation for disloyalty and charged with sounding the alarm when divinely decreed disaster was rapidly approaching and time for repentance was running out. Duguid likens the role of an OT prophet to air raid wardens of WWII who sounded an alarm when enemy bombers were approaching so people could rush to bomb shelters. Duguid also captures the irony of Ezekiel's situation: "the 'enemy' . . . is none other than God himself!"[12]

Tragically, many prophets were derelict in their duty and failed to fulfill their commission. Isaiah paints a sorry picture of watchmen who were blind, mute, loved to sleep, sought their own gain, and spent most of their time drinking beer! (Isa 56:10–12). Jeremiah and Ezekiel deliver scathing condemnation against prophets who "wag their own tongues and yet declare, 'The Lord declares.'" These self-proclaimed prophets "do not benefit these people in the least" (Jer 23:31, 32; Ezek 13). The hallmark of true prophets like Isaiah, Jeremiah, and Ezekiel lay in their faithfulness to watch and their willingness to warn.

Four Possible Outcomes

In 3:16–21 Yahweh outlines four possible scenarios resulting from Ezekiel's compliance or non-compliance to his commission. Each case study incorporates the form "if/when . . . then." Legal material in the Pentateuch contains similarly constructed case laws.[13] As soon becomes clear, the stakes are high—literally life and death.

10. 1 Sam 14:16; 2 Sam 13:34; 18:24; 2 Kgs 9:17–18, 20.

11. Isa 21:11–12; Ps 130:6. Today, for the benefit of observant Jews in Jerusalem, a siren signals the beginning of Sabbath on Friday at sunset.

12. *Ezekiel*, loc. 1575.

13. See, e.g., Exod 21:2—22:16; Lev 20.

- Case One: Wicked person not warned and does not repent
- Case Two: Wicked person warned and does not repent
- Case Three: Righteous person falls away and not warned
- Case Four: Righteous person falls away but warned and repents

From this it follows that if Ezekiel does his duty and warns the individual, whether wicked or righteous, of the consequences of disobedience, and they ignore it and continue in their sin, they alone are responsible for their sin and will die. Ezekiel will not be held accountable. If, however, he fails to warn either the wicked or righteous, then he will be held accountable for their death. In the case of the righteous person who lapses but when warned repents, he will live and Ezekiel "will have saved [himself]" (3:22).

This passage raises several perplexing questions. They can be laid out as follows:

- Why isn't there a case in which a wicked person repents and lives?
- What does it mean that the unrepentant will die?
- What does it mean for Ezekiel to be held accountable for the sinners' death?
- What bearing does this passage have on the controversial question of the perseverance of the saints?

The first two case studies suggest that none of the wicked repent. This, however, must be modified in light of chapters 18 and 33 in which we learn that a wicked person can indeed repent and live. "But if a wicked person turns away from all the sins they have committed and keeps all my decrees and does what is just and right, that person will surely live; they will not die" (18:21; cf. 33:12). Furthermore, Yahweh himself makes clear his attitude toward the wicked: "As surely as I live, declares the Sovereign Lord, I take no pleasure in the death of the wicked, but rather that they turn from their ways and live. Turn! Turn from your evil ways! Why will you die, people of Israel?" (33:11). Several NT passages make the same point: "The Lord . . . is patient with you, not wanting anyone to perish, but everyone to come to repentance" (2 Pet 3:9). "God our Savior . . . wants all people to be saved and to come to a knowledge of the truth" (1 Tim 2:4).[14]

But what does the expression "they will die" mean? Some say it refers only to physical death.[15] Others say spiritual death, that is, final separation of the soul from God at the last judgment.[16] It could, of course, include both. "The two uses of the word 'die' in verse 26 suggest first the physical and then the spiritual death."[17] I think both meanings are intended.

So, what about Ezekiel's accountability for non-compliance in his task as watchman, his giving account "for their blood" (2:18, 20). I think the meaning is that failure to carry out his duty as a watchman would lead to a loss of reward, not a loss of salvation. It is akin to Paul's description of a builder who builds on the foundation of Christ with the equivalent of wood, hay, or straw. In such a case, "the builder will suffer loss but yet will be saved—even though only as one escaping through the flames" (1 Cor 3:15).[18] What is clear is that if Ezekiel warns both the wicked and righteous of their sin, he has fulfilled his responsibility.[19]

14. Cf. Rom 11:14; 1 Tim 4:10; 2 Tim 2:25.

15. "Eternal death or the second death (Rev 20:14) is not in focus here. The judgment yet to come will determine that" (Stuart, *Ezekiel*, 42–43). "In these verses, God is not talking about loss of salvation but rather about physical death" (*Life Application Study Bible*, 1694).

16. See Wesley, *Works of John Wesley*, 10:242–44. "It remains, then, one who is righteous in the judgment of God himself, may finally fall from grace" (244).

17. Hall, "Ezekiel," 3:416.

18. See also 1 John 2:8: "Watch out that you do not lose what we have worked for, but that you may be rewarded fully."

19. "When the watchman warns the righteous, and the righteous heeds the warning, the watchman has delivered his own soul, i.e., he has fulfilled his responsibility" (Hall, "Ezekiel," 3:380).

Problem of Perseverance

The elephant in the room (i.e., the text) concerns the doctrine of eternal security. Can a righteous person fall away and be eternally lost? A full discussion of this controversial topic is well beyond the scope of my book. The issue, however, is of such importance I share my opinion.

I believe Scripture teaches the real possibility of apostasy resulting in loss of salvation. For an Israelite, apostasy meant turning away from the one true and living God and worshiping a false god (or gods). Ezekiel the watchman warns "members of the authentic covenant community, those who have in the past trusted in Yahweh and submitted to his lordship. The statement assumes that such persons . . . *can* turn from their righteousness . . . and be sentenced to death. . . . It is not how one begins the race that counts, but how one ends."[20]

In the NT, apostasy refers to one who initially trusts in Christ but then turns away and renounces him. In Paul's words, "If we disown him, he will also disown us" (2 Tim 2:12).[21] Whether a righteous person who commits apostasy may repent and return to fellowship with God is a moot point.[22] What isn't debatable is the danger of departing from faith in Christ. The Master spoke of those who "believe for a while, but in the time of testing they fall away" (Luke 8:11:13). Paul was afraid some of the Galatians "[had] been alienated from Christ" and had "fallen from grace" (Gal 5:4). He reminded Timothy "that in the later times some will abandon

20. Block, *Ezekiel*, 1:149. Italics his. In a footnote Block disagrees with Calvin that the righteousness involved "has only the outward appearance" (*Ezekiel*, 1:159). Block has another footnote in which he says "the statement is silent on Yahweh's effectual keeping power." But then he goes on to say, "On the possibility of genuine believers falling away, but the reality that God's grace prevents them from apostatizing, see M. J. Erickson, *Christian Theology* (Grand Rapids: Baker, 1985), pp. 992–97." (*Ezekiel*, 159). What kind of possibility is that? You can't have your cake and eat it too!

21. See also Heb 6:4–6; 10:26–31; 12:25.

22. This depends in part on one's interpretation of Heb 6:4–6 and 10:26. At face value these passages state the impossibility of repentance after apostasy. Shank argues that it is possible (*Life in the Son*, 309–29).

the faith" (1 Tim 4:1). The writer of Hebrews warned his readers against having "a sinful, unbelieving heart that turns away from the living God" (Heb 3:12).

For some, this generates great anxiety and fear. It shouldn't. Scripture teaches that those who trust in Christ will never be lost.[23] The key here is recognition that faith in Christ is a *condition* for eternal security. God doesn't believe for us nor infuse within us a predestined faith that inevitably *causes us* to trust in Christ to the very end.[24] Rather, "the one who stands firm to the end will be saved" (Matt 10:22 cf. 24:13). The apostle Peter encourages believers that their heavenly inheritance "is kept in heaven for [them]" (1 Pet 1:4). But in the next breath, reminds them of the indispensable condition: "who *through faith* are shielded by God's power until the coming of the salvation that is ready to be revealed in the last time" (1 Pet 1:5). The apostle Paul assures believers that if they continue to trust in Christ as Savior and Lord, they are not only shielded, they are invincible: "[Nothing] in all creation will be able to separate us from the love of God that is in Christ Jesus our Lord" (Rom 8:39).

While nothing *external* may separate us from God's love, something *internal* can—our own failure to continue trusting in the Savior.[25] That's why Paul regularly reminds his converts of this

23. "For my Father's will is that everyone who looks to the Son and believes in him shall have eternal life, and I will raise them up at the last day" (John 6:40); "Very truly I tell you, the one who believes has eternal life" (John 6:47); "I give them eternal life, and they shall never perish; no one will snatch them out of my hand. My Father, who has given them to me, is greater than all; no one can snatch them out of my Fathers' hand" (John 10:28–29). "When you believed, you were marked in him with a seal, the promised Holy Spirit, who is a deposit guaranteeing our inheritance until the redemption of those who are God's possession—to the praise of his glory" (Eph 1:13–14).

24. "We cannot be protected against ourselves in spite of ourselves" (Westcott, *St. John*, 158). "[T]he New Testament affirms that eternal life in Christ is our present possession only on the condition of a present living faith, rather than as the irrevocable consequence of a moment's act of faith sometime in the past" (Shank, *Life in the Son*, 63).

25. "Some passages aim to assure us of our 'security' from the forces that are against us. They do not mean to provide security against the consequence or possibilities of our own neglect, indifference, or unbelief" (Picirilli, *Understanding Assurance*, loc. 145).

necessity. "But now he has reconciled you . . . *if you continue in your faith*, established and firm, and do not move from the hope held out for you in the gospel" (Col 1:22–23). "Consider therefore the kindness of God: sternness to those who fell [unbelieving Jews], but kindness to you, *provided that you continue in his kindness.* Otherwise, you also will be cut off" (Rom 11:22).[26] Pastor John of Patmos adds this exhortation to believers undergoing severe persecution: "This calls for patient endurance and faithfulness on the part of God's people" (Rev 13:10; cf. 14:12). Trust and obey remains the standing order until Christ returns.

The prospect of persecution may unnerve us and generate fear lest our faith fail in the hour of trial. That's when we must lean on the promises of God and the powerful presence of the Holy Spirit. The apostle Paul assures the Colossians they are "being strengthened with all power according to his glorious might so that [they] may have great endurance and patience" (Col 1:11). He reminds the Ephesians that God "is able to do immeasurably more than all we ask or imagine, according to his power that is at work within us" (Eph 3:20). Bank on it, God supplies more than sufficient power—Paul calls it "his incomparably great power for us who believe" (Eph 1:19)—to enable each believer to stay the course *whatever the circumstances.*[27] Here is the bottom line: whosoever will may be saved and whosoever will may persevere to the end.[28]

ANOTHER THEOPHANY AND COMMISSIONING (3:22–27)

The conclusion of Ezekiel's call and commission involves another theophany. Yahweh instructed him to go out to the plain and

26. See also 1 Cor 10:12; 15:1–2; 2 Cor 13:5; Gal 5:4, 21.

27. "The believer in Christ begins a new life in a new probation; goes on his way with a habitual assurance; and thus is *animated to persevere to the end*. This is the New-Testament economy of the Christian life, to which it is everywhere faithful." (Pope, *Compendium*, 3:100 [italics added for emphasis]).

28. John 3:16; 4:14; Acts 2:21; Rev 22:17. In support of the position here argued, see also Duty, *If Ye Continue*; Marshall, *Kept by the Power*; Picirilli, *Understanding Assurance*; and Shank, *Life in the Son*.

receive more instructions. When he did so, the glory of Yahweh appeared as it had the previous week by the Kebar River. The repeat appearance of Yahweh's glory functions as a sort of booster shot fortifying the prophet against the rigors ahead.[29]

Like the first vision, the Spirit came into Ezekiel and raised him to his feet.[30] The Spirit then mandated restrictive conditions under which Ezekiel must perform his prophetic task. The limiting factors of Ezekiel's commission are as follows:

- Confined to his house
- Bound by ropes
- Rendered mute until Yahweh speaks to him.

Each of these restrictions is puzzling. Wright says this passage "plumbs the depths of paradox almost to the point of farce."[31]

- Why does Ezekiel shut himself inside his house? Isn't this counterproductive?
- Why do his fellow deportees tie him up with ropes and prevent him from going out among the people? What were they afraid of?
- Why does Yahweh impose muteness on his spokesperson except in response to a divine word? Doesn't this greatly hinder his role as a watchman?

Much attention has been devoted to making sense of this passage.[32] Some interpret the text metaphorically as a communal ban placed on his prophetic activity. Others resort to theories of textual

29. A metaphor suggested by the worldwide COVID-19 pandemic and the importance of getting a booster shot to protect against the virus and its variants.

30. Cf. 1:28; 2:2.

31. *Ezekiel*, 69. Zimmerli calls this passage "one of the most difficult passages in the whole book" (*Ezekiel*, 158). Block lists no fewer than nine problems requiring investigation (*Ezekiel*, 1:152).

32. See a brief discussion in Blenkinsopp, *Ezekiel*, 32. For an extended treatment see Block, *Ezekiel*, 1:151–61.

corruption or displacement. Still others focus on some supposed mental illness, such as aphasia (total or partial loss of speech). Taking the text at face value, I offer these comments.

First, Yahweh tells Ezekiel to shut himself inside his house (3:24). This is not metaphorical, but it does seem counterintuitive. How can he function as "watchman for the people of Israel" (3:16) while hunkering down in his home?[33] But as it turns out, community elders regularly frequent his home with the expectation of hearing a word from Yahweh.[34] Though they may not like what they hear, they keep coming, perhaps hoping the prophet will change his tune.

One thinks of the apostle Paul when he was under house arrest at Rome awaiting his trial before Nero. "For two whole years Paul stayed there in his own rented house and welcomed all who came to see him. He proclaimed the kingdom of God and taught about the Lord Jesus Christ—with all boldness and without hindrance!" (Acts 28:30–31). Paul marveled at God's hand in all this: "Now I want you to know, brothers and sisters, that what has happened to me has actually served to advance the gospel" (Phil 1:12). In short, both Ezekiel and Paul discovered that the sovereign God can easily accomplish his purposes in spite of adverse and limiting circumstances.

Secondly, the tying up with ropes is not metaphorical. The community elders probably did this, but for what purpose and for how long remains obscure. It may be that, initially, they sought to restrain him from publicly delivering messages of judgment upon Jerusalem because it undermined the morale of the exiles, who hoped against hope for an eventual return home. Jeremiah even endured punishments and imprisonments on account of his oracles of judgment upon Jerusalem and the temple.[35] Less likely is the suggestion that because of Ezekiel's bizarre behavior the elders were afraid he might be dangerous to others. Whatever the

33. Stuart assumes that Ezekiel performed his symbolic act outside his house in view of the residents (*Ezekiel*, 51).

34. See Ezek 8:1; 14:1.

35. Jer 20:1–2; 36:5, 19; 37–38.

explanation, he was able to perform his symbolic actions depicting the siege of Jerusalem inside his house.[36]

Thirdly, Ezekiel's muteness apparently was not total. When Yahweh spoke to him, he broke his silence and delivered his message to the elders. In his daily routine, however, he apparently uttered not a word. Ezekiel's behavior reminds us of Jeremiah's antisocial behavior in connection with weddings and funerals.[37] In his dealings with his prophets, the sovereign LORD sometimes employs unconventional means to accomplish his purpose.[38]

When Yahweh spoke to Ezekiel, the divinely imposed muteness was temporarily suspended and the prophet proclaimed the message. There was, however, no guarantee that the people would listen because "they are a rebellious people" (4:27). Nonetheless, the prophet's preaching carried with it a "whosoever will" invitation. Those addressed by the divine word could choose either to listen or to refuse. As already indicated, the stakes were high—nothing less than life or death. One is reminded of a similar hour of decision in the Apocalypse of John: "Let the one who does wrong continue to do wrong; let the vile person continue to be vile; let the one who does right continue to do right, and let the holy person continue to be holy" (Rev 22:11). The reality of genuine freedom of choice in salvation history is writ large on the pages of the sacred text. Why anyone would refuse life, however, remains shrouded in mystery.

36. Block says "Ezekiel is never seen out on the streets or in the marketplace" (*Ezekiel*, 1:161). But as Wright observes, "The limited audience for the performance itself doesn't limit its effectiveness since the whole community will know before nightfall what happened at Ezekiel's house that day" (*Ezekiel*, 74).

37. See Helyer, *Jeremiah*, 45–46.

38. One thinks of Isaiah's nakedness (Isa 20:2–3) and Jeremiah's wearing a yoke made of straps and crossbars (Jer 27–28).

CONCLUSION

The prophetic phenomenon that best explains Ezekiel's divinely mandated confinement is the symbolic act. Prophets employed sign-acts to convey unpalatable messages to unreceptive audiences. By means of street mime, prophets like Isaiah and Jeremiah communicated judgment oracles without even uttering a word—their actions spoke louder than words.[39] By means of his confinement and restrictions, Ezekiel acts out the plight of the doomed inhabitants of Jerusalem during Nebuchadnezzar's siege of Jerusalem in 588–86 BC.

The first three chapters of Ezekiel's book narrate his call, commission, and installation into the office of prophet. In this section he is:

- Cautioned about his audience's hardness of heart
- Confronted with the seriousness of his task
- Commanded to tell the people what Yahweh tells him to say
- Confined to his house

The stage is set for one of the most dramatic series of sign-acts ever performed by a Hebrew prophet or anyone else for that matter. Taken together they portray one of the most horrifying episodes in Jewish history.

39. See further Helyer, *Yesterday*, 274–77; Helyer, *Jeremiah*, 39–57.

4

Symbolic Siege of Jerusalem

This was no party and certainly no fun at all.

—Christopher J. H. Wright

INTRODUCTION

Chapters 4 through 7 paint a grim picture of Jerusalem and Judah's fate. Ezekiel delivers the bad news by means of an extended symbolic action and two judgment oracles that put a fine point on what was already graphically clear.

Ezekiel's elaborate pantomime, a "prophetic theater of the absurd,"[1] is structured by two Yahweh oracles giving specific instructions for its performance (4:1; 5:1). The two judgment oracles that follow are introduced by a standard messenger formula: "The word of the Lord came to me" (6:1; 7:1) and concluded with a formulaic expression punctuating not only this section but the entire

1. Blenkinsopp, *Ezekiel*, 33. Wright titles 3:16—5:17 "theatre of the doomed" (*Ezekiel*, 64).

book: "Then they will know that I am the Lord" (6:14; 7:27). The performance unfolds in three distinct acts.

ACT ONE: JERUSALEM UNDER SIEGE (4:1–3)

The stage props for this divine screenplay are relatively simple but highly effective. First, Ezekiel is ordered to sketch a map of Jerusalem on a clay block or slab. Mud bricks were easily accessible in Babylon because all buildings, whether public or private, were constructed from this abundant resource.[2] Since Ezekiel was quite familiar with the layout and features of Jerusalem, he etched from memory an outline of the city. The elders who witnessed this bizarre scene, with Ezekiel acting as if he were the commander of an invading army and directing the siege, easily recognized the familiar layout of Jerusalem.[3]

Ezekiel adds more stage props to his enactment. These include a siege wall around the perimeter, a siege ramp, camps for the invading army, and battering rams. Most ominously, Ezekiel places an iron pan between himself and the city. He then pretends to launch an all-out assault upon the city, as if he had reverted to his childhood days and were playing toy soldiers. "This will be a sign to the people of Israel" (4:3). The elders got the point; their beloved city was about to be besieged. The only question was, would it miraculously survive as it had over a hundred years earlier in the days of Hezekiah?[4] Ezekiel's "iron wall" dispels any hope of divine intervention—the city is doomed.

2. In contrast, cities in Israel were typically built of limestone. Even today, municipal codes in Jerusalem require that buildings be faced with Jerusalem limestone.

3. Trying to provide a plausible chronological sequence for the sign acts in chs 4–5 has proven to be a challenging puzzle. See Block, *Ezekiel*, 1:167–70 for his attempted solution. I forgo such an attempt and simply focus on the meaning of each discrete symbolic act.

4. This was the famous siege by Sennacherib in 701 BC. For the circumstances see 2 Kgs 18:17—19:27.

ACT TWO: BEARING SIN AND UNDERGOING STARVATION (4:4–17)

Setting the Stage

The next phase of his symbolic act stretches out to more than a year—430 days to be exact. First, he lies on his left side for 390 days, during which time he bears the sin of Israel, here referring to the northern kingdom. Then, he shifts over to his right side and bears the sin of Judah. The days are explained as representing years of sin. Adding action to a relatively static spectacle, Ezekiel bares his arm and prophesies against his inert model. Further drama is added by the notice that he is tied up with ropes during this long ordeal.

What follows next is truly appalling. He adheres to a severely limited subsistence diet, that is, eating just enough to stay alive. He bakes his daily bread from a mixture of grains and legumes amounting to twenty shekels or about eight ounces. His liquid intake amounts to about two-thirds of a quart per day. As you can imagine, the bread ration is of very poor quality—a smorgasbord of ingredients—though providing just enough calories to survive.

An interesting moment occurs when Yahweh instructs him to bake his bread over human excrement. At this our priestly prophet pushes back: "Not so, Sovereign Lord, I have never defiled myself. From my youth until now I have never eaten anything found dead or torn by wild animals. No impure meat has ever entered my mouth" (4:14). Yahweh permits a substitution, namely cow dung. Just a comment here. The reader may not know that cow dung can in fact serve as fuel. American families making the arduous trek on the Oregon Trail resorted to the abundant dried dung of buffaloes littering the Great Plains as fuel for their cooking fires.

Try to picture what happens to Ezekiel—he literally shrivels up and wastes away. After some fourteen months, he looks like a Holocaust survivor. This is the most shocking symbolic action ever performed by a Hebrew prophet. In short, it enacts the fate of the

Jerusalemites—they will slowly starve to death. Yahweh's word of explanation to Ezekiel says it all: "They will be appalled at the sight of each other and will waste away because of their sin" (4:17).

Stating the Significance

So, what's the meaning? The main point of the prophet's protracted pantomime seems clear enough but the details are problematic. What about the 390 days the prophet lay on his left side and the additional forty days on his right? One can make the numbers match the respective histories of the northern and southern kingdoms only by a generous rounding off.[5] The total of 430 years however, corresponds exactly to the years the Hebrews spent in slavery in Egypt (Exod 12:40–41) suggesting that Ezekiel's sign-act recalls the beginnings of Israel's story as state slaves in Egypt and forecasts their impending exile in Babylon because of their many sins. The longer period for the northern kingdom of Israel may point to the longer duration of covenant violations.

But did Ezekiel actually lie twenty-four-seven on his left and right sides for 430 days tied up with ropes? It's hard to imagine. More likely, he spent a portion of each day acting out his prophetic drama, including having someone tie him up with ropes.[6] Since he had to prepare his daily allowance of food and drink, not all his time was spent besieging the model city.

It goes without saying that Ezekiel's symbolic act was the talk of the town and drew a steady stream of onlookers to his house. Periodically, the prophet received a divine oracle and delivered it to his "captive audience."

Finally, what are we to make of the expression "bear the sin of Israel/Judah"? We may safely rule out any notion of vicarious

5. For attempts to do this see Block, *Ezekiel*, 1:177–78.

6. "It is unlikely that Ezekiel lay on his side continuously for 390 days. He probably adopted this posture for several hours each day, timing his lying down to achieve maximum rhetorical effect, this is, at the busiest part of the day" (Block, *Ezekiel*, 1:179).

atonement in Ezekiel's acted parable.[7] Only Yahweh's servant in Isa 53 was ordained to be a sin-bearer in that sense.[8] But OT priests did offer sacrifices for sin and in a metaphorical sense bore the sins of the people. In his symbolic act, however, Ezekiel does more than that, he actually bears the consequences of the sins of Israel and Judah *in his own body*. His painful sufferings were on display for over a year and previewed the horrors soon to be visited upon the doomed inhabitants of Jerusalem. The impact on those who watched can scarcely be imagined.

There is something about this extraordinary sign-act that is not immediately obvious but which deserves reflection. In light of the NT, Ezekiel's acted parable foreshadows the work of Christ on our behalf. In the words of the apostle Peter, "He [Christ] himself bore our sins *in his body* on the cross so that we might die to sins and live for righteousness" (1 Pet 2:24). Of course, Christ did infinitely more than *symbolize* bearing sin; he actually *atoned* for the guilt of sin "not only for ours but also for the sins of the whole world" (1 John 2:2).[9] We will have further occasion to draw attention to typological links between Ezekiel and Jesus.

ACT THREE: BARBERSHOP THEOLOGY (5:1–17)

The next phase of Ezekiel's elaborate sign-act focuses on a barber's razor and what Ezekiel does with the hair clippings. After, or perhaps during, his 430-day starvation stint, the emaciated prophet performs five distinct actions pantomiming the destiny of Jerusalem's inhabitants:

1. He cuts off all the hair of his head and beard.[10]

7. "Ezekiel's action cannot be interpreted as expiatory. Neither prophet nor priest in the OT ever fulfilled this role" (Block, *Ezekiel*, 1:177).

8. Isa 53:5–12.

9. Rom 3:24–26; 5:1–11.

10. Wright is puzzled: "Where Ezekiel got a sword from in a community of exiles is a mystery" (*Ezekiel*, 83). In my view, there is no mystery at all. A sword was a necessary item for a wide range of activities and the exiles were settled in the area of Tel Aviv as part of a development project. The exiles, after all, were

2. He divides the clippings into three equal parts by means of a scale
3. He places the hair piles inside the model and proceeds to burn one third, strike with a sword another third, and scatter the remaining third in the wind.
4. He takes a few hairs and tucks them into the folds of his garment.
5. He takes a few of these and burns them up in the fire.

Three divine oracles, which Ezekiel is permitted to deliver audibly, remove any ambiguity about the pantomime. The model city is "Jerusalem, which I have set in the center of the nations" (5:5).[11] This description implies Israel's special mission: to bear witness to the only true and living God to all the nations and peoples. To this end the patriarchal stories, the account of the rise of the Davidic dynasty, the hymnody of Israel, and the prophetic oracles all testify.[12]

The great tragedy was Israel's failure in carrying out her divine mission. Not only did Israel disobey Yahweh's decrees; she even failed to live up to the standards of the surrounding pagan nations. For this reason, she will indeed bear witness to the nations—not as an example to follow but as a warning to heed.

---

not living in the equivalent of a POW camp and possession of a sword hardly posed a threat to the Babylonians.

11. Based on this text, the rabbis spoke of Jerusalem as "the navel of the earth." The book of Jubilees described Mount Zion as in the midst of the navel of the earth (*OTP* 2:73). This notion was taken up by Christians and may be visually appreciated in the venerable Church of the Holy Sepulcher. In the Catholicon, the Roman Catholic chapel opposite the Edicule (the ornate monument built over the traditional tomb of Christ), is a chalice called the omphalos, i.e., the navel. In medieval Christian tradition it was deemed fitting that the place where Christ was crucified, buried, and rose again should be located at the very center of the earth. A striking example of this is the famous Mappa Mundi in Hereford Cathedral. This map of the whole known world places Jerusalem right at the center. For a wonderful interactive version of the map, see https://www.themappamundi.co.uk/mappa-mundi/.

12. See Gen 12:2–3; 1 Sam 17:26; 1 Kgs 8:41–43; Pss 67; 96; 117; Isa 43:10; 44:8; 49:6.

The third oracle spells out in more detail the consequences of Israel's rebellion against Yahweh's conditions and stipulations for enjoying the blessings of the Sinai Covenant. The revelation that Yahweh will personally intervene in the ensuing judgment and the unparalleled degree of pain inflicted is startling: "I myself will do to you what I have never done before and will never do again" (5:8).

But there is a limit to the duration of Yahweh's anger and there is a positive outcome: "They will know that I the LORD have spoken in my zeal" (5:13). In the short run, however, the punishments inflicted and endured will be *horrific*, even involving cannibalism within families ("parents will eat their children and children will eat their parents" [5:10]). Nor will the ultimate sanction of the Sinai covenant—namely, expulsion from the land—provide any respite from affliction. The neighbors among whom they live will add insult to injury by hurling accusations and treating them as "an object of horror" (5:15). For the majority of dispersed Jews, the dark night of exile would not be a time of happiness and joy.

THEOLOGICAL REFLECTION

Christians need to pay careful attention to this passage. The NT repeatedly warns believers not to play fast and loose with their covenant Lord. To be sure, the NT church of Jesus Christ is not composed of one ethnic people nor is it constituted as a theocracy as in the OT. But the worldwide, multi-ethnic, multi-lingual, multi-racial people of God under the new covenant are obligated to obey its stipulations. In the words of the covenant Lord, "If you love me, keep my commands" (John 14:15). Deliberate and persistent violation of these standards puts one in spiritual peril.[13]

The apostle Paul doesn't mince words when addressing the possible consequences of continuing to live under the control of the flesh (the old nature): "I warn you, as I did before, that those

13. See Heb 2:12–14; 4:1–2; 6:4–8; 10:26–31; 12:15–17, 25–29.

who live like this will not inherit the kingdom of God" (Gal 5:21).[14] The author of Hebrews (someone in the Pauline circle) is even more explicit: "If *we* deliberately keep on sinning after *we* have received the knowledge of the truth, no sacrifice for sins is left, but only a fearful expectation of judgment and of raging fire that consume the enemies of God" (Heb 10:26–27). To be excluded from the New Jerusalem will not be a time of happiness and joy.

Let's speak frankly: believers may also experience the consequences of divine punishment for national sins that cry out to the heavens. I'm thinking of the many thousands of believers during the American Civil War who were killed in combat or died of wounds and disease. The national sin of slavery brought down God's "terrible swift sword" upon the entire populace, be they believers or not. During the 2020–22 pandemic, many believers have perished. Without presuming to know exactly why God allowed COVID-19 to take so many lives here and abroad, I affirm without hesitation, "Yes, Lord God Almighty, true and just are your judgments" (Rev 16:7). Those who truly trusted in Christ and perished are "with Christ, which is better by far" (Phil 1:23).

PREACHING TO THE MOUNTAINS (6:1–14)

In one of the more striking soliloquies in Scripture, Ezekiel was instructed to "prophesy against the mountains" (6:1). As we will see later, he prophesies to an even more improbable audience in his famous chapter 37. Ezekiel's monologue in chapter 6 personifies the hill country of Israel and in so doing indicts its inhabitants for covenant disloyalty. Their egregious violation of the first and second commandments is singled out as the primary reason Yahweh "has been grieved by their adulterous hearts, which have turned away from me" (6:9). Because they "deliberately keep on sinning after [they] have received the knowledge of the truth, no sacrifice for sins is left, but only a fearful expectation of judgment and of raging fire that will consume the enemies of God" (Heb

14. See also 1 Cor 6:9–11; Eph 5:5–7.

10:26–27). And so, Yahweh wields his terrible swift sword against the mountains of Israel. Though not directly mentioned, Nebuchadnezzar king of Babylon, like Sennacherib the Assyrian, will unwittingly serve as "the rod of my anger in whose hand is the club of my wrath!" (Isa 10:5).

The consequences, already graphically clear in the sign acts of chapters 5 and 6, are now restated in stark prose. The prophet, relaying Yahweh's words, drives home three main points.

1. The Irony and Justice of Israel's Judgment (6:1–7)

All the hilltops populated with altars and idols dedicated to false gods were destined for destruction in the coming Babylonian invasion. It's not that the Babylonians were opposed to polytheism, since they had a large pantheon of gods and goddesses. Smashing and ruining a conquered nation's gods, however, demonstrated the superiority of the Babylonian gods and of course the empire that sponsored and worshiped them. Besides the ideological and political propaganda value, the ruined idols, typically wood figures overlaid with gold and silver, were of some value since they could be melted down for the royal coffers.[15]

The destruction of the high places and their idols was accompanied by a massacre of the Israelite citizenry. The Israelite gods proved impotent to deliver them from Babylonian blood lust. Ironically, by abandoning the only true God for false gods, their bodies are stacked like cordwood in front of their idols. It's as if their corpses were offered up as burnt offerings. In short, their punishment fits the crime. An oft-repeated refrain in Ezekiel, occurring some sixty times, concludes the first point: "and you will

15. One thinks of Jeremiah's classic parody on idolatry: "For the practices of the peoples are worthless; they cut a tree out of the forest, and a craftsman shapes it with his chisel. They adorn it with silver and gold; they fasten it with hammer and nails so it will not totter; . . . they must be carried because they cannot walk. Do not fear them; they can do no harm *nor can they do any good*" (Jer 10:3–5).

know that I am the Lord" (6:7). Divine judgment is no mere slap on the wrist.

2. A Land Is Wasted (6:14)

But human inhabitants are not the only ones who experience Yahweh's wrath—even the mountains of Israel fall prey to devastation. "And I will stretch out my hand against them and make the land a desolate waste from the desert to Diblah—wherever they live" (Ezek 6:14). Israel's repeated violation of covenant obligations removed the shield of divine protection and opened the gates to the Babylonian hordes who burn and pillage everything, resulting in an almost uninhabitable environment.

It bears mentioning that our modern environmental crisis is largely owing to human sinfulness, namely, covetousness, exploitation, and selfishness. Original sin despoiled paradise; continuing sin despoils the planet.[16]

3. A Remnant Is Spared (6:8–10)

In the sign act of the razor, Ezekiel was instructed to put a few hairs of his head in the folds of his garment. Only a remnant will survive the sword and be "scattered among the lands and nations" (6:8). Yahweh's chastisement, however, achieves its intended purpose: the scattered remnant remembers him and they "loathe themselves for the evil they have done" (6:9). This recovered self-awareness leads to the theological truth running throughout the book like a scarlet thread: "And they will know that I am the Lord" (6:10). Despite grievous violations of their covenant obligations, they cannot escape their divine destiny: to be a light to the gentiles and a blessing to all peoples on earth as Yahweh originally promised Abram.[17]

16. Gen 3:17–19; Jer 4:22–26.

17. See Isa 42:6; 49:6, and Gen 12:3.

Israel's dispersion to the ends of the earth meant that its central creed, the Shema, went with them. "Hear O Israel: The LORD our God, the LORD is one" (Deut 6:4). The unity of God and his demand for justice ("Do what is right and good in the LORD's sight . . ." [Deut 6:18]) served as a continuing witness to the gentiles.[18] Furthermore, as a consequence of the Abrahamic covenant, the Jewish contribution to civilization has been incalculable and out of all proportion to their numbers. The fine arts, business, industry, law, music, medicine, science, and technology, to name but a few areas of human endeavor, have all been enriched by Jewish genius. Yahweh always keeps his covenant promises.

ANNOUNCING THE END (7:1–27)

Ezekiel, like a watchman on the wall, blows his trumpet and shouts the alarm. "The end! The end has come" (7:2; cf. 7:3, 5, 6, 7, 10, 12). In poetic verse he announces imminent catastrophe. No safe place can be found, no stratagem devised, no hope entertained, no ransom offered: "not one of them will preserve their life" (7:13). They are doomed and must face a grim fate. In cadences reminding us of the prophet Amos, Ezekiel equates "the end" with "the day," an abbreviated version of a frequent expression in prophetic literature, "the day of the LORD."[19] This time period can refer either to a historical judgment, as in chapters 6 and 7, or to the eschatological judgment, as in chapters 38–39.[20]

18. In the NT we read of gentiles who were attracted to the ethical monotheism of Judaism and formed a significant group called "God fearers." They participated in and sometimes financially supported the synagogue (Luke 7:1–5). Many God fearers accepted the gospel and became Christians. See, e.g., Acts 8:26–39; 10:1–48; 16:13–15; 17:4; 18:7.

19. See Helyer, *Yesterday*, 294–302.

20. Sometimes a particular, *historical* judgment—for example, a locust plague (Joel 1:15)—morphs into an *eschatological* judgment (Joel 2:11).

Yahweh's Justice in Judgment

Yahweh's judgment imposed on the land of Israel accords with their conduct and detestable practices—a refrain repeated five times.[21] In short, they are getting precisely what they deserve and Yahweh will not show pity or spare them.

Israel's Moral and Political Collapse

Like his eighth-century predecessor Isaiah and his contemporary Jeremiah, Ezekiel strips away the veneer of prosperity and religiosity and lays bare the rotten soul of a nation. "The land is full of bloodshed, and the city is full of violence" (7:23), evoking the characterization of the pre-flood generation.[22] Ezekiel, like a doctor, reads his patients' vital signs and delivers a devastating diagnosis: you're going to die!

There is no remedy because society is irreversibly dysfunctional. In a revealing analysis of their frantic attempts to save themselves from the coming disaster, they turn to the traditional institutions and sources of guidance, but in vain. They search "for a vision from the prophets, and priestly instruction in the law . . . and counsel of the elders" (7:26). Alas, there is no vision, no instruction, and no counsel. Effective political leadership no longer exists. No wonder "the hands of the people of the land will tremble" (7:27).

Nonetheless, Ezekiel summons the people "Prepare chains!" (7:23). Most interpreters understand this as a command to the invaders and as a preview of the grim reality facing the survivors—chained together in a long train and led off into exile.[23] It

21. 7:3, 4, 8, 9, 27.

22. "Now the earth was corrupt in God's sight and was full of violence" (Gen 6:11).

23. See Block, *Ezekiel*, 1:267; Alexander, *Ezekiel*, 779; Taylor, *Ezekiel*, 96. Walton refers to Egyptian reliefs depicting captives bound by chains. "Captives are usually depicted in Egyptian and Mesopotamian art bound in chains. This is the case in a relief found in the Ramesseum at Thebes picturing Asiatic, Ethiopian, and central African captives being paraded before Rameses II. A

may, however, refer to a desperate measure to thwart the breaching of the city wall. The argument goes like this: chains would be laid along the outside base of vulnerable sections of the wall and covered from view. When the invading army rolled their battering ram up to the wall, the defenders would suddenly pull the chains up and thereby deflect the ram, rendering it ineffective. This stratagem of course would only work once since the defenders were unable to venture out and lay the chains again. As I have written elsewhere, "it is clearly a counsel of despair, since the doom of the city is certain."[24] It simply delayed the inevitable—a breach in the wall and a massive influx of soldiers bent on killing, looting, and rape. On either interpretation, those who survived the carnage were chained together and marched off to exile

The national disaster achieves its purpose, something Ezekiel never tires of reminding his audience: "Then they will know that I am the Lord" (7:27). Yahweh's intention is always redemptive not revengeful. He takes no pleasure in the death of the wicked.[25]

So, was there any hope that the ultimate covenant curse would be stayed at the last moment? Recall that Isaiah beseeched his countrymen of the eighth century: "'Come now, let us settle the matter, says the Lord. Though your sins are like scarlet, they shall be as white as snow, though they are red as crimson, they shall be like wool. *If you are willing and obedient*, you will eat the good things of the land, but *if you resist and rebel*, you will be devoured by the sword. For the mouth of the Lord has spoken" (Isa 1:18–20). Jeremiah likewise threw out a lifeline to his fellow Judeans: "Reform your ways and your actions, and I will let you live in this place" (Jer 7:3). For some time, Jeremiah ignored reality and clung to the false hope of an eleventh-hour reprieve. Yahweh slammed the door shut. "Even if Moses and Samuel were to stand before me, my heart would not go out to this people" (Jer 15:1). The divine

similar scene of captive Canaanite and Philistine prisoners is carved into the wall of the mortuary temple of Rameses III at Medinet Habu." ("Ezekiel," on 7:23).

24. Helyer, "Queries and Comments," 18.

25. Ezek 18:23.

verdict was inevitable and irreversible: "Those destined for death, to death; those for the sword, to the sword; those for starvation, to starvation; those for captivity, to captivity" (Jer 15:2).

Ezekiel knew the point of no return had been reached: "The end has come!" (Ezek 7:2). Ironically, "the most wicked of nations" will be "a rod to punish the wicked" (7:11). Yahweh's punishment fits the crime. And it certainly wouldn't be fun.

5

Secret Surveillance of the Sanctuary

They may have tied him up, but they couldn't tie him down.

—Christopher J. H. Wright

INTRODUCTION

Chapters 8–11 form a unit and narrate a remarkable, even unparalleled, visionary experience.[1] The Spirit of Yahweh transports Ezekiel to the Jerusalem temple where he observes what is happening in its sacred precincts. Yahweh then informs him what is going to happen to the temple, city, and land as a consequence of the "utterly detestable things the Israelites are doing" (8:6). This all unfolds while he sits in his home at Tel Aviv with the elders seated before him.

Translation in the Spirit is a rare phenomenon in Scripture. In the OT Elijah experienced something similar.[2] In the NT the

1. Block, *Ezekiel*, 1:280.

2. Obadiah, Ahab's palace administrator and a faithful Yahwist, said to Elijah: "I don't know where the Spirit of the Lord may carry you when I leave you" (1 Kgs 18:12).

evangelist Philip was apparently snatched up bodily and transported from somewhere near Gaza to Azotus (Ashdod).[3] But nothing really compares with Ezekiel's spiritual levitation and flight to Jerusalem. So, add another bizarre achievement to Ezekiel's already bizarre credits.

JEREMIAH AND EZEKIEL: FELLOW TRAVELERS

Before delving into details, I draw attention to the many intertextual links between Jeremiah's temple sermon and Ezekiel's visionary visit to the temple.[4] For example, Jeremiah's temple sermon and Ezekiel's temple visit both denounce Judah's sin in similar language: "Son of man, do you see what they are doing—the utterly detestable things the Israelites are doing here" (Ezek 8:6). Jeremiah accuses his listeners of apostasy in the sanctuary: "They have set up their detestable idols in the house that bears my Name and have defiled it" (Jer 7:30). Ezekiel's symbolic action in which he cuts off his hair (Ezek 5:1–4) recalls the conclusion of Jeremiah's temple sermon: "Cut off your hair and throw it away; take up a lament on the barren heights, for the Lord has rejected and abandoned this generation that is under his wrath" (Jer 7:29).

The following chart highlights more similarities between these two sixth-century prophets of Yahweh.

Jeremiah	Ezekiel
Visionary Call: branch of an almond tree and a boiling pot tilting toward Judah (Jer 1:11–14).	*Visionary Call:* the throne-chariot of Yahweh (Ezek 1:4–28).

3. Acts 8:39–40. Gaza is about twenty-two miles from Azotus. I'm leaving out of consideration accounts of bodily translation to heaven or paradise such as Enoch (Gen 5:24; cf. *1 En.* 1:9), Elijah (2 Kgs 2:11), Paul (2 Cor 12:1–4), and John (Rev 4:1–2).

4. Intertextuality refers to connections or allusions shared by two separate literary works.

Commission: Get yourself ready! Stand up and say to them whatever I command you" (Jer 1:17).	*Commission:* "Son of man, stand up on your feet and I will speak to you. . . . I am sending you to the Israelites, . . . you must speak my words to them." (Ezek 2:1, 3, 7).
Watchman: "Sound the trumpet, . . . raise the signal, . . . take warning, Jerusalem. . . . Listen to the sound of the trumpet! Look an army is coming" (Jer 6:1, 8, 22).	*Watchman:* "I have made you a watchman for the people of Israel; so hear the word I speak and give them warning from me." (Ezek 3:17).
Eating the word of Yahweh: "When your words came, I ate them; they were my joy and my heart's delight." (Jer 15:16).	*Eating the word of Yahweh:* "Eat this scroll. . . . So I ate it, and it tasted as sweet as honey in my mouth" (Ezek 3:1, 3).
Temple sermon (Jer 7).	*Temple visit* (Ezek 8–11).
Symbolic acts: the linen belt (Jer 13), celibacy (Jer 16), the potter and the pot (Jer 18–19), wearing a yoke (Jer 27–28), and buying a field (Jer 32).	*Symbolic acts:* enacting a siege (Ezek 4), cutting off his hair (Ezek 5), portraying deportation (Ezek 12), no public mourning for his wife (Ezek 24), the two sticks (Ezek 37:15–27).

Though separated by distance, these two stalwart spokespersons share much in common. We shouldn't be surprised—the Spirit of Yahweh speaks through both and they both confront listeners in denial concerning the impending crisis.

EZEKIEL'S VISIONARY VISIT

Ezekiel's visionary tour of the Jerusalem temple unfolds in five acts.[5]

Act One: Detestable Things in the Sanctuary (8:1–18)

September 17, 592 BC, fourteen months after Ezekiel's initial call and commission vision, the elders of Tel Aviv gathered in his

5. Block arranges the material in a tight, chiastic fashion (*Ezekiel*, 1:272).

house. Perhaps they were hoping for a more encouraging word after hearing Ezekiel utter the alarming announcement, "The end has come!" (7:1). But no hopeful word was forthcoming.

Instead, the Spirit of Yahweh came upon Ezekiel and he immediately went into a visionary trance. The first thing he saw was "a figure like that of a man" (8:2) but a man unlike any other, a man robed in the brightness of fire and glowing metal. Once again, he beheld "the glory of the God of Israel" (8:4). It was Yahweh himself who stretched out his hand and seized the prophet by his hair—it had grown back since he shaved it off—and the Spirit of Yahweh lifted Ezekiel up "between heaven and earth" (8:3) and instantly transported him to Jerusalem, a distance of some six hundred miles the way the crow flies. What a ride!

First Stop: Idol of Jealousy

Acting as a tour guide, Yahweh first takes Ezekiel to the entrance of the north gate. "Son of Man, look toward the north" (8:5). What Ezekiel saw was a blatant violation of the first and second commandments of the Sinai covenant, an idol conspicuously located right at the north entrance.[6]

The idol is not identified, but it may have been an image of Baal, the old Canaanite fertility god, or his female consort Asherah. This morally depraved religion was never totally eradicated from the hearts and minds of Israelites and when kings reigned who were not loyal to their covenant obligations, its degrading rituals seeped back into society like sewer gas.[7] Alas, this is just the tip of an iceberg: "But you will see things that are even more detestable" (8:6).

6. Exod 20:3–6. Notice especially the line "for I, the LORD your God, am a jealous God" (v. 5).

7. Even though the godly king Josiah led a reform movement to rid the land of such practices, they lay dormant until his faithless son Jehoiakim succeeded him and turned a blind eye to their resurgence. Jeremiah saw through the hypocrisy and feigned piety of the leadership and common people early on in Josiah's reign. See Helyer, *Jeremiah*, 9, 11.

Second Stop: Seventy Elders Practicing Secret Idolatry

Yahweh next leads Ezekiel to the court entrance. Another weird episode. Ezekiel sees a hole in the wall and Yahweh tells him to dig into the exposed wall behind the hole. After digging through the wall, he sees a doorway admitting him to an interior room, a secret chamber. Once inside, an appalling sight greets him. "In the darkness," seventy elders including Jaazaniah son of Shaphan were worshiping "all the idols of Israel" (8:12). Each elder was standing before a shrine of their self-chosen god holding a censer from which a fragrant incense arose. To borrow a Pauline idiom, what they were really doing was spreading "an aroma that brings death" (2 Cor 2:16).

The apostates excuse their actions: "The Lord does not see us; the Lord has forsaken the land" (8:12). Both assertions reveal an appalling ignorance of who Yahweh is and what he requires of his covenant people. How tragic that one of the ringleaders was Jaazaniah, whose father Shaphan served as secretary of state under the godly king Josiah.

Once again, we are faced with a sobering reality. Faith is not like heredity; it can't be passed on to our offspring. Faith requires a free, personal decision to trust in the Lord God of Israel and a commitment to obey his commandments. Jaazaniah joins a long list of sons who departed from the faith of their fathers: Eli, Samuel, and David are but a few parents who agonized over their wayward sons.

In our day of social media, it's trendy for sons and daughters to proudly proclaim their departure from faith in Christ with blogs and tweets that go viral, encouraging skeptics and dismaying believers. Sometimes the prodigals come home; often they don't. No heartache is more painful for parents than watching a child fall away; no joy is greater than having them come home. "Let's have a feast and celebrate. For this son [or daughter] of mine was dead and is alive again; he [or she] was lost and is found" (Luke 15:24).

This passage requires further comment. How are we to interpret Ezekiel's temple tour? Is it in real time or imaginary time?

I wonder if Dickens took a page from Ezekiel when he wrote *A Christmas Carol*. Like Ezekiel, Ebenezer Scrooge, thanks to conveyance by the Ghost of Christmas Past, is able to review scenes from his happy childhood and early adult years. He observes but is unobservable. The Ghost of Christmas Present forces him to witness his callousness and miserly behavior affecting everyone around him, especially his own family and the Cratchit family. Finally, the Ghost of Christmas Yet to Come enables Ebenezer to eavesdrop negative comments about a rich man who had died. When Scrooge requests the identity of the person, he is taken to a graveyard and shown his own tombstone, completely shattering his contempt and prompting deep contrition. The story of Scrooge has a happy ending because he repents and reforms his ways. We don't know how the story of Jaazaniah turns out, but one suspects it wasn't a happy ending.

In my view, we are not talking about real time in Ezekiel's surveillance—real time being defined as the simultaneous occurrence of an event and its perception by an observer. Ezekiel's visit takes place "in visions of God" (8:3) and so, much like a dream, he can dig through a wall, be rapidly repositioned in different locations, and witness undetected what is happening.

Third Stop: Women Worshiping Tammuz

Can it get worse than that? Yes, it can. "You will see them doing things that are even more detestable" (8:13).

Yahweh takes Ezekiel to "the entrance of the north gate of the House of the Lord" (8:14) where he witnesses women engaged in idolatrous worship, performing a mourning ritual for the Babylonian god Tammuz. This cult actually goes back to an ancient Sumerian myth about Dumuzi who died and descended to the underworld. Dumuzi's lover and consort Inanna (Babylonian "Ishtar") went in search of him and "in the course of time [he] rose from the realm of the dead to new life with the rebirth of the vegetation."[8] The myth reflects the annual cycle of nature in which during the winter months everything goes dormant and then comes to life again in the spring.

This pagan cult appealed to women because Tammuz was a fertility god enabling fecundity and fruitful harvests. What it reveals is a view of nature infused with gods—a sad departure from belief in one, self-existent God who created all things and is the only source of life and blessing. When the mothers of Judah resort to pagan magic the floodgates open and society drowns in a spiritual abyss.

It would seem the descent into apostasy could sink no lower. But tragically, we've not reached the bottom of the barrel yet. "You will see things that are even more detestable" (8:13).

Fourth Stop: Twenty-Five Men Worshiping the Sun

The fourth and final stop brings us to the very entrance to the temple. If one plots the course of Ezekiel's stops, Yahweh moves him each time from one degree of sanctity to a higher one. He now arrives at a very high degree of holiness, where only priests were permitted, between the portico of the temple itself and the altar. In this sanctified place, Ezekiel the priest observes the most shocking sacrilege of all.

Twenty-five men with their backs to the temple were bowing down to the sun arising in the east. Wright captures the affront with this memorable line: "Metaphorically, sunnies to the east; moonies to the LORD. The insult is blatant and breathtaking."[9] What utter foolishness that Shamash, the Assyrian sun god, usurps Yahweh, the one who created the sun.[10] As Allen points out, this provocation of Yahweh "provides the final scaffolding for a literary framework borrowed from [Deuteronomy]."[11] "They made him

8. Blenkinsopp, *Ezekiel*, 55.

9. Wright, *Ezekiel*, 107.

10. Shamash was an ancient Mesopotamian sun god. In Hebrew the cognate word for the sun is *shemesh*. The formerly Canaanite town of Beth Shemesh incorporates the name of this god, literally, "House of the Sun (god)."

11. Allen, *Ezekiel 1–19*, 145.

jealous with their foreign gods and angered him with their detestable idols. They sacrificed to false gods, which are not God—gods they had not known, gods that recently appeared, gods your ancestors did not fear" (Deut 32:16–17).

During his reforms, Josiah stamped out the astral worship installed by the apostate king Manasseh.[12] But Josiah's reform movement was short-lived and after his death it resurfaced with a vengeance. Jeremiah railed against Judah's apostasy: "You, Judah, have as many gods as you have towns; and the altars you have set up to burn incense to that shameful god Baal are as many as the streets of Jerusalem" (Jer 11:13). The women were equally guilty in this defection because they "knead the dough and make cakes to offer to the Queen of Heaven" (Jer 7:18), a reference to the astral deity Ishtar, the goddess associated with the planet Venus.[13]

Yahweh's question to Ezekiel highlights the tragic state of affairs: "Have you seen this, son of man? Is it a trivial matter for the people of Judah to do the detestable things they are doing here?" (Ezek 8:17). It is not trivial and neither is the divine response: "I will deal with them in anger; I will not look on them with pity or spare them" (v. 18).

Act Two: Divine Judgment Begins in the Sanctuary (9:1–11)

The eleventh hour has passed and the clock now strikes midnight. In his visionary trance Ezekiel witnesses the destruction of his beloved city and temple. Yahweh summons six angelic agents of divine punishment (described as six men). A seventh, carrying a writing kit, accompanies them; he is charged with a very important task: "put a mark on the foreheads of those who grieve and lament over the detestable things that are done in it" (9:4).[14]

12. "In the two courts of the temple of the Lord, he [Manasseh] built altars to all the starry hosts" (2 Kgs 21:5).

13. The sun god, Shamash, together with the moon god, Sin, and the planet goddess, Ishtar (Venus), formed an astral triad.

14. On the later traditions of identifying the righteous by placing a mark on their foreheads, see Block, *Ezekiel*, 1:310–14.

The good news is that a righteous remnant still remains loyal to Yahweh. This reminds us of a similar remnant in the dark days of Elijah, when seven thousand did not bow down and kiss an image of Baal (1 Kgs 19:18). The theme of a righteous remnant runs throughout Scripture.[15]

The image of the destroying angels alludes to two prior occasions in which angelic agents were deployed to execute divine judgment. The first was during the foundational experience of Israel, the exodus from Egypt. On that occasion, during the tenth plague, all the firstborn of Egypt, whether human or animal, were put to death, from Pharaoh's household all the way down to "the prisoner in the dungeon" (Exod 12:29). All except the Israelites were divinely protected from "the destroyer" (Exod 12:23) by dabbing the blood of a lamb on the sides and tops of their doorframes. "The blood will be a sign for you on the houses where you are, and when I see the blood, I will pass over you. No destructive plague will touch you when I strike Egypt" (Exod 12:13).

A second judgment involving a destroying angel occurred in the days of King David. His pride-filled desire to know the size of his army resulted in a three-day plague carried out by the angel of the LORD. The final tally was devastating: seventy thousand people perished "from Dan to Beersheba" (2 Sam 24:15). Only Yahweh's intervention spared Jerusalem from utter disaster. The only silver lining of this terrible judgment cloud was David's purchase of the site where the first temple was eventually built, the very place where Yahweh stayed the hand of the destroying angel.[16]

But now an even darker cloud descends upon Israel. After marking the righteous remnant on their foreheads, the six destroying angels sweep through the city, beginning at the temple. Like grain before a scythe, the corpses of "the old men, the young men and women, the mothers and children" (9:6) pile up in the temple courtyard, the scene of "all the detestable things." The six destroying angels, each armed with a deadly weapon, enter through the

15. It begins with Noah who "found favor in the eyes of the LORD" (Gen 6:3).

16. For background of this story see Helyer, *David*, 175–76.

north gate and stand beside the bronze altar, the place of animal sacrifice, except that now the people of Jerusalem become the holocaust, the whole burnt offering.[17]

It was more than Ezekiel could bear. Like his contemporary Jeremiah, who actually lived in Jerusalem at the time, Ezekiel cried out to Yahweh for mercy upon the remnant.[18] But neither stay of execution nor passing over the houses of the righteous would be granted.[19] They too would perish alongside the wicked, the latter brazenly and stupidly insisting, "The Lord does not see" (9:9). The clock had run out and the limit of forbearance exceeded: "The sin of the people of Israel and Judah is exceedingly great. . . . I will bring down on their own heads what they have done" (9:10).

Act Three: Departure of the Shekinah from the Sanctuary (10:1–22)

Prior to the divine judgment on Jerusalem, the glory of Yahweh departs. Like a solemn funeral recessional, the throne-chariot bearing the Shekinah slowly moves eastward from the threshold of the temple, to the temple courtyard, to the eastern gate of the temple mount, and then to the Mount of Olives. Ezekiel breaks off his narrative at that point; presumably, the glory of God disappears into the heavens.[20]

17. Archaeological evidence of the conflagration that reduced most of Jerusalem to ashes has turned up during excavations of the City of David and the western hill. "The archaeological evidence . . . can be counted among the most dramatic at any biblical site. . . . In addition, many of the buildings . . . were also destroyed in a fierce conflagration" (Shiloh, "Jerusalem," 2:709).

18. See Jer 14:19–22.

19. Yahweh did, however, preserve Jeremiah through the holocaust of 586. Baruch, Jeremiah's faithful assistant and scribe, also survived the siege. See Helyer, *Jeremiah*, 13–15.

20. Connecting the dots, I call attention to the fact that on the Mount of Olives Jesus ascended into heaven in the presence of his apostles (Luke 24:50–53; Acts 1:9–12). Some forty days prior to his ascension Jesus warned his disciples that both temple and city would be destroyed (Matt 24:2; Luke 21:20). Forty years later Jesus' prophecy was literally fulfilled. According to

The divine exodus portends disaster because "the divine king has abandoned his residence."[21] Without the presence of Yahweh to defend the city and its temple, the people are powerless to resist Nebuchadnezzar's war machine. As in the days of Eli the high priest, we've reached another Ichabod moment: "the Glory has departed from Israel" (1 Sam 4:21, 22). Just as the ark of the covenant was captured and the city of Shiloh burned to the ground, so, too, the temple and Jerusalem would be reduced to ashes and a majority of its population would die by sword, starvation, and disease.[22]

Will the glory of God ever return? Stay tuned for a remarkable reappearance.

Act Four: Death of Pelatiah at the Eastern Gate of the Sanctuary (11:1–13)

We backtrack for a moment. Before the glory of Yahweh departs to the Mount of Olives, Ezekiel witnesses one more judgment scene. This time it concerns twenty-five leaders of Judah who were pillaging the people and pocketing ill-gotten gains. Their attitude is summed up in an arrogant boast, "Haven't our houses been recently rebuilt? This city is a pot, and we are the meat in it" (11:3).[23] Imagining themselves as choice pieces of meat securely stored in a pot, all the while expropriating the property of others, they are in for a rude awakening.[24]

The Spirit of Yahweh instructs Ezekiel to prophesy against them for their wicked plots and cold-blooded murders. Apparently,

Jewish tradition the destruction of both the first and second temples occurred on the same calendar day.

21. Block, *Ezekiel*, 1:327.

22. See Jer 15:2.

23. This kind of behavior was exhibited by the kings of Judah during the years before the invasion, most notably in Jehoiakim, whom Jeremiah assailed for his self-centered life of luxury at the expense of his people. See Helyer, *Jeremiah*, 10–11.

24. The interpretation of this passage is problematic. See Block, *Ezekiel*, 1:332–34 and Allen, *Ezekiel 1–19*, 160.

they attempted to flee the country during the invasion but were apprehended at the borders, tortured, and executed by the sword. Ironically, they were indeed choice pieces of meat and their enemies devoured them with relish. Their sentence was just: "And you will know that I am the Lord, for you have not followed my decrees or kept my laws but have conformed to the standards of the nations around you" (11:12).

As Ezekiel was prophesying, Pelatiah one of the evil leaders died. This so unnerved the prophet he again pleaded with Yahweh: "Alas, Sovereign Lord! Will you completely destroy the remnant of Israel?" (11:13). The divine answer was immediate and unequivocal: No, there is a future for the remnant.

Act Five: Deliverance of the Remnant in Yahweh's Sanctuary (11:14–25)

The people of Jerusalem have a calloused, self-centered approach to the exiles such as Ezekiel: "They are far away from the Lord; this land was given to us as our possession" (11:15). Wrong on both counts! In the first place, as Ezekiel knew from firsthand experience, the Holy God of Israel was very much present in unholy Babylon. Secondly, it's the dispersed remnant who hold the right to the land, not the rebellious inhabitants "whose hearts are devoted to their vile images and detestable idols" (11:21).

In a stunning reversal of fortunes, the present Jerusalem sanctuary and its largely apostate worshipers will undergo massive destruction and death, while the scattered remnant discover that wherever they go, Yahweh is "a sanctuary for them" (11:16). Note here an intimation of the NT teaching whereby the people of God now constitute a spiritual temple in which the Spirit of God dwells.[25]

In his visionary visit to Jerusalem, Ezekiel hears Yahweh's promise of restoration for the scattered remnant. Jeremiah,

25. See Eph 2:19–22; 1 Pet 2:4–5.

incarcerated within the doomed city, has a dream in which he too hears a similar message of hope.[26] The table below shows the parallels.

Ezekiel	Jeremiah
"I will gather you from the nations and bring you back from the countries you have been scattered, and I will give you back the land of Israel again" (Ezek 11:17).	"I will bring my people Israel and Judah back from captivity and restore them to the land" (Jer 30:3).
"I will give them an undivided heart and put a new spirit in them; I will remove from them their heart of stone and give them a heart of flesh" (Ezek 11:19).	"I will put my law in their minds and write it on their hearts" (Jer 31:33).
"Then they will follow my decrees and be careful to keep my laws" (Ezek 11:20).	"They will all know me from the least of them to the greatest" (Jer 31:34).
"They will be my people and I will be their God" (Ezek 11:20).	"I will be their God and they will be my people" (Jer 31:33).

Jeremiah calls this new relationship between Yahweh and his people "a new covenant" (Jer 31:31) and "an everlasting covenant" (Jer 32:40; 50:5); Ezekiel describes the same reality as "an everlasting covenant" (Ezek 16:60) and "a covenant of peace" (34:25). But as we will see, Ezekiel's unique contribution to the new-covenant concept includes a new temple and new priesthood.[27] Even though Jeremiah and Ezekiel were prophets of the calamity and collapse of Judah, they both foresee a glorious future for Israel and Judah.

Ezekiel's visionary experience concludes on an uplifting (!) note. When the throne-chariot lifts off from within the city and hovers over the Mount of Olives to the east, the Spirit lifts Ezekiel up and transports him back to his home in Tel Aviv. He had a lot to tell the exiles and tell them he did—"everything the LORD had shown me" (11:25).

26. Jer 31:26.

27. Ezek 40–48.

Footnote to the Vision (12:1–28)

Though chapters 8–11 is a unit, chapter 12 functions as an exclamation point to the vision and dispels any lingering false hopes about the future of Jerusalem and Judah. In accordance with Yahweh's command, the prophet performs another powerful symbolic action making it crystal clear what's going to happen to the city and its royal family.

Ezekiel roleplays the plight of survivors in Jerusalem. During daylight hours, he packs a few personal belongings in a sack and leaves his house. Then, in the evening, with just enough light so the neighbors can observe, he digs a hole through the wall of his house and crawls out with his bag over his shoulder. As he does so, he covers his face "so he cannot see the land," picturing the emotional pain of people who will never return to their homeland (12:6).[28] In Rembrandt's famous painting *Jeremiah Lamenting the Fall of Jerusalem* (1630), one can see Zedekiah, the last king of Judah, leaving the doomed city with his arm over his face, unable to bear the thought of never seeing it again. Wall reliefs from the palace of the Assyrian King Sennacherib at Nineveh actually depict Jewish survivors of the siege of Lachish being marched off to exile. One can see men, women, and children carrying sacks over their backs just like Ezekiel depicts in his symbolic action.

Adding one more dramatic effect to an already all-too-vivid depiction, Ezekiel eats his food and drinks his water with trembling and shuddering. To this he adds a word of explanation: "They will eat their food in anxiety and drink their water in despair" (12:19).

One final nail in the coffin must be hammered home. The Judean inhabitants of the homeland keep their spirits up by mindlessly reciting two sayings: "The days go by and every vision comes to nothing" (12:22) and "The vision is for many years from now, and he prophesies about the distant future" (12:27).[29] Ezekiel

28. See 2 Kgs 25:4–7; Jer 39:2–7; 52:7–11.

29. In Jerusalem itself Jeremiah contradicted similar slogans: "This is the temple of the Lord" and "we are safe" (Jer 7:4, 10). See further Helyer, *Jeremiah*, 24. Ezekiel is aware of the scuttlebutt back home because there was communication between the diaspora communities and the homeland. See Ezek 24:26; Jer 29:1–3.

dashes all such false hopes: "It will be fulfilled without delay . . . in your days" (12:23, 25). The fate of their beloved city is both sealed and soon.

Thus ends the first portion of Ezekiel's prophecy. The reader knows what will happen. The departure of the glory of God from his city and temple because of the detestable things taking place portends imminent destruction. Only a remnant will survive the onslaught. But the story isn't finished: a refrain recurs throughout this section: "Then you will know that I am the LORD" (12:20). No date is set for this realization, but it's certain—Yahweh says so.

6

Allegories and Announcements of Judgment

Second only, perhaps, to the genealogies in 1 Chronicles, the lurid allegories of Ezekiel 16 and 23 must qualify as the chapters in the Bible least likely to be read aloud in church—and just as unlikely to be preached from. They are long, they are lewd, and the language in places is, frankly, pornographic.

—Christopher J. H. Wright

INTRODUCTION

Ezekiel is unique in several ways. Here is another instance; he alone employs allegories to convey his judgment oracles.[1] In

1. Perhaps we should qualify this and add Zechariah's word about the two shepherds and two staffs. See Zech 11:4–17. Another qualification concerns the appropriateness of labeling these passages as allegories. Modern scholars tend to prefer the designation extended metaphor. On this point see Kelle, *Ezekiel*, 42, 179–83.

fact, we have five such allegories, each of which conveys an unpalatable, even shocking message.

JERUSALEM: FUEL FOR FIRE (15:1–8)

The first allegory, though devoid of sexual overtones, is nonetheless appalling in its content. It begins with three rhetorical questions, each easily answered by Ezekiel's listeners and readers. The point is this: do grape vines have any use beyond bearing and nurturing the grape clusters that grown upon them? The answer is no. They aren't useful as pegs or even charcoal. In short, they are "not useful for anything" (15:5). They can, however, be burned up and that is precisely what is going to happen to the people of Jerusalem (15:6).

One hears echoes of this passage in Jesus' allegory of the vine and branches in John 15. He warns his disciples about failing to abide in him: "I am the vine; you are the branches. If you remain in me and I in you, you will bear much fruit; if you do not remain in me, you are like a branch that is thrown away and withers; such branches are picked up, thrown into the fire and burned" (John 15:6). Both testaments repeatedly sound an alarm against those who break faith with their covenant Lord.

Yahweh's reason for such treatment is straightforward: "they have been unfaithful" (11:8). This explanation is the keynote for the allegories that follow, allegories that jar the reader by their explicit sexual imagery. Like symbolic actions, Ezekiel's allegories attract attention.

AN ADULTEROUS WIFE (16:1–63)

Ezekiel drops all subtlety in the next allegory. It's an "in-your-face" condemnation of Jerusalem.[2] Like Jeremiah's temple sermon, Ezekiel resorts to a history lesson to drive home his point.[3] Although

2. Duguid, *Ezekiel*, 209. Duguid prefers to call this an extended metaphor since it doesn't quite fit the usual designation of allegory.

3. Jeremiah reminds his listeners that in the days of Eli the high priest,

presented in allegorical terms, Ezekiel's listeners could easily decode its meaning. Unfolding in five stages, it's a story about a broken vow and amazing grace.

1. A Pitied Foundling

In this metaphorical discourse, Jerusalem is pictured as a faithless bride and Yahweh is the ever-faithful husband. A brief ancestry precedes a birth narrative. Ancient Jerusalem traced its beginnings to both Amorite and Hittite ancestors. This mixed pagan parentage presages the unfolding story of Hebrew Jerusalem. "Like parents, like children."

In Ezekiel's extended metaphor, as a newborn babe, Jerusalem was despised (cord not cut, not washed in water, rubbed with salt, and wrapped in cloths) and destined to die in the open field (16:5). But an amazing divine intervention transpires. Yahweh passes by and sees the plight of the foundling. He determines she will survive: "I said to you, 'Live!'" (16:6).

2. A Privileged Wife

Yahweh not only cared for the foundling, he nurtured her and in time married her ("you became mine"). As his bride Yahweh lavished her with love and luxury. She became "very beautiful and rose to be a queen" (16:13). In fact, her fame spread to the surrounding nations.

Let's pause a moment and unpack Ezekiel's extended metaphor. Behind Jerusalem lies the story of Israel's humble beginnings and struggle to survive, first in Canaan, then in Egypt as state slaves, then in the "vast and dreadful wilderness" of Sinai, and finally back in Canaan surrounded by Amorites, Canaanites, and Philistines. But in accordance with Yahweh's plan, David captured

---

Yahweh allowed the Philistines to destroy Shiloh where the ark of the covenant was housed (Jer 7). In fact, the Philistines even captured the ark and kept it for a time (1 Sam 4–6).

Jerusalem from the Jebusites, established it as his capital, and subdued the surrounding nations. In the halcyon days of Solomon, the fame of Jerusalem was known throughout the ancient east and the known world.

3. A Promiscuous Wife

At this point the story goes south. At the apogee of Israelite power, Solomon, inexplicably, opens the floodgates of idolatry (1 Kgs 11). Subsequently, apostasy and syncretism inundate the land. A privileged wife becomes a promiscuous wife. In fact, she even engages in prostitution, but of an unheard-of kind; she chases after lovers and pays to have sex with them. As the allegory makes clear, the primary meaning of prostitution in this context has to do with infidelity to the one, true God. Of course, pagan idolatry with its licentious rituals, spills over into the lives of its adherents and becomes sexual adultery as well. A series of lovers—Egypt, Assyria, and Babylonia—take advantage of a "nymphomaniac bride."[4]

Yahweh, the aggrieved husband, is outraged: "You adulterous wife! You prefer strangers to your own husband!" (16:32). She is indicted for a long litany of offenses, descending to the barbarous depths of child sacrifice.[5] Yahweh has no alternative. She must face the consequences of persistent infidelity.

4. A Punished Prostitute

This passage raises serious concerns about the way in which Yahweh and women are portrayed. Let's briefly consider each matter in turn.

In Ezekiel's allegory, Yahweh acts like a sadistic wife-abuser who in a fit of rage permits his unfaithful spouse's illicit lovers to murder her ("I will bring on you the blood vengeance of my wrath and jealous anger. Then I will deliver you into the hands of your

4. Blenkinsopp, *Ezekiel*, 76.

5. "The indictment [is] one of the longest in the prophetic literature" (Blenkinsopp, *Ezekiel*, 78).

lovers, and they will tear down your mounds and destroy your lofty shrines. They will strip you of your clothes and take your fine jewelry and leave you stark naked. They will bring a mob against you, who will stone you and hack you to pieces with their swords" (Ezek 16:38–40). This is truly shocking.[6] But we need to remind ourselves that this literary device runs counter to the consistent portrayal throughout Scripture of Yahweh's character and behavior as compassionate, forgiving, and loving ("But you, Lord, are a compassionate and gracious God, slow to anger, abounding in love and faithfulness," Ps 86:15, etc.). In fact, Yahweh doesn't directly inflict torture on his wife here; rather, what he does is *remove his care and protection from her*. As she has abandoned him for her lovers, he passes her over to their "care." In this regard, Ezekiel echoes Isaiah's indictment of Israel and Judah in his well-known song of the vineyard (Isa 5). Likening his people to a choice vine planted in a prime location, Yahweh is bitterly disappointed when they fail to produce good grapes even though lavished with tender, loving care. He decides to "take away its hedge, . . . break down its wall," and "command the clouds not to rain on it" (Isa 5:5–6). Yahweh's vineyard is now open to invaders and trespassers (surrounding nations) who destroy and trample. Ezekiel makes the same essential point by using graphic sexual imagery.

Regarding the woman's hyper-promiscuity, Ezekiel's portrayal of Jerusalem *is* pornographic, but also *atypical*. That is, Ezek 16 is an exception to the generally positive depiction of female sexuality in the OT. In this story Ezekiel deliberately intended to shock his audience by an unheard-of aberration, not to suggest that all females were like the nymphomaniac he sketched in his allegory.

In short, the shocking imagery employed by Ezekiel to describe both Yahweh and his unfaithful wife falls in line with his shocking, symbolic actions—he is aiming to arrest the attention of his listeners!

That brings us to another important observation. There is more going on here than the downward spiral of a depraved

6 "How does one respond to such troublesome portrayals of God?" (Block, *Ezekiel*, 1:468).

prostitute-like wife. In fact, this is not about a literal woman at all. Behind the metaphor lies national unfaithfulness to Yahweh and entanglement in political alliances. These illicit liaisons with neighboring powers involve Judah in a catch-twenty-two situation. Because Zedekiah's government broke its treaty with the Neo-Babylonian Empire, they had to face the wrath of Nebuchadnezzar, who marched to Jerusalem and wreaked vengeance upon his rebellious vassal. As it turned out, the horrific siege of 588–86 witnessed atrocities much like the punishments meted out to Ezekiel's metaphorical, unfaithful wife.[7] In other words, the real-life military consequences of Judah's clash with Babylon have crept back into the imagery of Ezekiel's story, blurring the boundary between the adulteress metaphor and the national situation. This blurring has the effect of making the story unlike literal cases of response to adultery. This is, in part, why the violence depicted seems so disproportionate to the offence. It also indicates that Ezekiel's story has its limits and needs to be read with care.

Ezekiel depicts Jerusalem as an unfaithful mother who has two wayward daughters: Samaria (the northern kingdom of Israel), and Sodom (the southern kingdom of Judah). The older daughter breaks her vows with Yahweh first with "detestable practices,"[8] but her younger sister's actions are even "more depraved" (16:47).

The sin of Sodom and her daughters is so scandalous it makes Samaria and her daughters "appear righteous!" (16:52) Note carefully the taproot of Sodom's sin: "She and her daughters were arrogant, overfed and unconcerned; they did not help the poor and needy." To this they added "detestable things" (16:50).

One thinks of the apostle Paul's analysis of sinful humanity. He traces the downward spiral into depravity back to this fundamental sin: "they neither glorified God nor gave thanks to him, but their thinking became futile and their foolish hearts were darkened" (Rom 1:21). Samaria and Sodom illustrate just how far one

7. Television images of atrocities and war crimes committed by Russian troops upon the civilian population of Ukraine remind us that international law has not restrained human depravity during war.

8. See 1 Kgs 12:25–33.

can fall into depravity when gratitude is replaced with greed. If Ezekiel were alive today, he would be appalled.[9]

5. A Pardoned Wife

The story seems to have a really bad ending. But Yahweh passes by again. This time he vows, "I will restore the fortunes of Sodom and her daughters and of Samaria and her daughters . . . and [they] will return to what [they] were before" (16:53, 55). A broken vow gives way to a renewed vow. "I will remember the covenant I made with you in the days of your youth, and I will establish an everlasting covenant with you" (16:60).

How can this be? Faith in the covenant-keeping God and genuine repentance leads to a new heart: "You will know that I am the Lord." But notice what precedes this acknowledgment. "Then, when I make atonement for you for all you have done, you will remember and be ashamed and never again open your mouth because of your humiliation, declares the Sovereign Lord" (16:63). Yahweh takes the first step. Then, in response to his undeserved, saving action on their behalf, they return to their covenant-keeping God.[10] In canonical context, this anticipates the once-for-all sacrifice of the Lord Jesus Christ for the sins of the world on the cross.[11] Looking beyond this climactic midpoint of salvation history, the apostle Paul anticipates the day when "the natural branches" will be grafted back into the olive tree and "all Israel will be saved" (Rom 11:21–23; 26).[12] Amazing grace!

9. Ezekiel's critique "has lost none of its relevance in our contemporary society" (Blenkinsopp, *Ezekiel*, 79).

10. In theological language, God's prevenient grace makes it *possible* for the sinner to respond in faith to his gracious offer (italics mine). "In a manner similar to Wesley's prevenient grace, the book [of Ezekiel] maintains the tension of initiative and gift—a human capacity to change through repentance, as Yahweh's Spirit reveals human need and empowers human response" (Kelle, *Ezekiel*, 214).

11. See John 1:29; 1 John 2:2; Rev 5:9–10; Heb 9:11–15; 10:12–13.

12. For the notion of the cross being the midpoint of salvation history, see Ladd, *Theology*, 65–67.

BARBECUE THEOLOGY (24:1–14)

Summer time is grilling time. And grilling season begins with an unpleasant, preliminary task. All the accumulated residue from the previous season should be scoured off lest it ruin the taste of the new season's meat. Employing a cooking song, Ezekiel depicts Yahweh the grill master performing this distasteful task in which Jerusalem is likened to an encrusted pot.[13] Yahweh decides to melt away the impurities with intense fire. Behind this vivid metaphor lies the reality of Jerusalem's wretched condition: rampant bloodshed and lewdness (adultery and idolatry).

Yahweh's attempts to scorch the pot failed: "It has frustrated all efforts; its heavy deposit has not been removed, not even by fire" (24:12). His people are impervious to all attempts to clean their sin-encrusted souls. He has no choice: "The time has come for me to act. . . . You will be judged according to your conduct and your actions, declares the Sovereign LORD" (24:14).[14]

DEATH AND DESTRUCTION (24:15–27)

Ezekiel's life is suddenly shattered—Yahweh gives him a heads up but that hardly softens the blow. The word from Yahweh may have come during the night, as he slept beside his wife. "Son of man, with one blow I am about to take away from you the delight of your eyes" (24:16). Adding to the emotional pain of this announcement, Yahweh forbids him to show any outside signs of mourning; no lamenting, no weeping, no tears, just quiet groaning. He must dispense with the traditional mourning customs (24:17) and this runs so countercultural as to be nothing short of scandalous.[15]

13. See Blenkinsopp, *Ezekiel*, 103.

14. I skip the allegories of the two eagles and a vine and the two adulterous sisters since they essentially repeat what has already been depicted in the other allegories.

15. Ancient and modern Near Eastern culture expresses grief in very emotional and outward ways.

No prophet was called upon to perform such an emotionally wrenching symbolic action. To be sure, Hosea went through a painful divorce and Jeremiah was forbidden to marry, mourn, or show sympathy at a funeral, and "enter a house where there is feasting" (Jer 16:1, 5, 8).[16] But Ezekiel is unique in that the death of his wife and his public reaction to it function as a sign-act.[17]

There is no mention of children. Like Jeremiah and the Suffering Servant of Isaiah, Ezekiel has no offspring to perpetuate his family name. There is, however, an important qualification regarding the Servant. "After he [the Servant] has suffered, he will see the light of life and be satisfied" (Isa 53:11)[18] and "*he will see his offspring*" (Isa 53:10). This promise is fulfilled in the countless multitude of spiritual children who become part of Messiah Jesus' great family.[19] In this sense, we can also speak of Jeremiah and Ezekiel's spiritual children, the righteous remnant. They heard the prophetic word, responded to Yahweh's gracious invitation, and received a new heart. In this regard, Jeremiah and Ezekiel were like the apostle Paul, who spoke of the Corinthian believers as his spiritual children (1 Cor 4:15).

The next morning Ezekiel spoke to the people. That evening his beloved wife died. The following morning he buried her and carried out Yahweh's instructions by not publicly mourning. The reaction of bystanders was immediate. "Why are you acting in this way?" (24:19). Another grim prophecy. The prophet's muted mourning mimes that of the Jerusalemites' during the siege. The magnitude of the loss of life in the midst of starvation, disease, and sheer terror precludes public mourning—only private grieving for deceased loved ones is possible.

16. "We have here, in a few short verses, one of the most poignant moments in the rich history of Israel's prophets—comparable to, but possibly surpassing, the heartbreak of Hosea and the loneliness of Jeremiah" (Wright, *Ezekiel*, 214–15).

17. One should also mention righteous Job who, in one fell swoop, lost all his wealth, seven sons, and three daughters—but not his wife. In fact, she later bore him seven more sons and three more daughters (Job 42:13).

18. The NIV translation is based upon 1QIsaa col. XLIV (Isa 52:13—54:4).

19. See Rom 8:16–17; Heb 2:10; Rev 7:9.

What's shocking in Ezekiel's explanation of his sign-act is the parallel between the death of his wife, "the delight of [his] eyes," and the destruction of the Jerusalem temple, "the delight of [their] eyes, the object of [their] affection" (24:21, 25). That which is dear either dies (Ezekiel's wife) or is destroyed (the Jerusalem temple). And like Ezekiel, the surviving Jerusalemites will not publicly mourn, just inwardly groan in their grief.

Ezekiel's oracle ends with a sign authenticating his prophecy: "on that day a fugitive will come to tell you the news" (24:26). Simultaneously, Ezekiel's silence ceases and he speaks with the bearer of bad news (24:27). Just as Yahweh said, so it happened. "In the twelfth year of our exile, in the tenth month on the fifth day, a man who had escaped from Jerusalem came to me and said, "the city has fallen!" Now the evening before the man arrived, the hand of the Lord was on me and he opened my mouth before the man came to me in the morning. So my mouth was opened and I was no longer silent" (33:21–22). That night was remarkable: Yahweh gave Ezekiel six oracle-visions, each introduced by the phrase "the word of the Lord came to me."[20] Together they unveil the end-time events leading to the grand climax of redemptive history. But more on that later.

The survivor reached Tel Aviv on January 8, 585 BC, five months after the temple was burned on August 14, 586. This latter date, *Tisha B'av* (the 9th of Av, according to the Hebrew calendar), is still remembered by observant Jews with a day of fasting. Incredibly, the temple that stood in Jesus' day was destroyed by the Romans on the same calendar date. In fact, several tragic events in Jewish history occurred on or near this same date.[21]

20. Ezek 33:23; 34:1; 35:1; 36:16; 37:15; 38:1. See Alexander, "Fresh Look," 158.

21. "In 1492 Columbus sailed the ocean blue." So the jingle goes. But as Columbus set out from Spain looking for a passage to India, Queen Isabella issued a decree on the 10th of Av that all Jews must leave the kingdom. A majority journeyed eastward and settled in the Balkans, Poland, and Russia. This region became the largest concentration of Jews in the world until the cruel policies of the Czars led to a massive emigration to the United States. This is the background of the musical *Fiddler on the Roof*. Other tragedies include the

HOLDING THE NATIONS ACCOUNTABLE (25:1—32:32)

This is both a turning point and a tension point in Ezekiel's book. The prophet postpones his amazing salvation oracles for Israel in chapters 33–48 by first inserting chapters 25–32, judgment oracles against the surrounding nations, especially Egypt and Tyre. This delay technique is also utilized by the apostle John in his apocalypse.[22]

Surprisingly, Babylon doesn't receive a judgment oracle. This is in contrast to Jeremiah, who severely condemns the capital city of the Babylonian empire. One wonders if this was because Ezekiel was an exile in the land of Babylon. If word should get out that he was condemning the government, he could be arrested and executed, which is precisely what happened to Ahab and Zedekiah, who were prophesying false hopes among the exiles.[23] The exiled apostle John disguises his woe oracle against Rome using the codeword "Babylon" in its place (Rev 18:9–24) and the apostle Peter substitutes Babylon for Rome in his letter to exiles from the capital of the empire (1 Pet 1:1; 5).

Following in the prophetic footsteps of Amos, Isaiah, Zephaniah, and Jeremiah, Ezekiel devotes considerable attention to Yahweh's judgment upon the surrounding nations.[24] This should not

destruction of Betar, the last Jewish fortress to fall in the Bar Kochba Revolt in AD 135, the start of the First Crusade in AD 1096 in which ten thousand Jews in Europe were massacred, the expulsion of Jews from England in 1290, and approval to implement "the final solution" of the Nazis, setting in motion the extermination of over six million Jews in death camps. This unspeakable act is often called the Holocaust (meaning "burnt offering"), though Jews usually refer to it as the Shoah (meaning "catastrophe").

22. Delays and interludes occur throughout the book of Revelation (e.g., ch. 7; chs. 12–14; chs. 17–18).

23. See Jer 29:20–23. "Ezekiel could not foretell the downfall of Babylon without the most serious danger to him and his hearers" (Ellison, *Ezekiel*, 100). Block, however, thinks "this absence may undoubtedly be attributed to the prophet's pro-Babylonian stance in political matters (*Ezekiel*, 2:4). I have my doubts about this explanation.

24. See Amos 1–2; Isa 13–24; Zeph 2:4–15; Jer 46–51.

be attributed to a narrow-minded nationalism that regards Israel superior to all other nations. Rather, these oracles establish a theological reality which must be taken with utmost seriousness. There is but one true and living God, the God of Israel, who is also God of all peoples and unto whom all nations are accountable, not least the people chosen to bear witness to this incomparable God.[25]

Ezekiel's oracles against the nations also convey a pastoral word of encouragement to the faithful remnant, both in Judah and Babylon. The atrocities committed by surrounding nations against Yahweh's people will not pass unnoticed.[26] Yahweh, the God of all nations, will pass judgment upon oppressors. Beyond the day of judgment, however, lies a day of blessing: "No longer will the people of Israel have malicious neighbors who are painful briers and sharp thorns. Then they will know that I am the Sovereign LORD" (28:24).[27] Dark clouds still loom on the prophetic horizon, but beyond them lies the dazzling glory of Yahweh's triumphant return to his restored land and reconciled people. A new day will dawn and springtime return because Aslan is back.[28]

25. A point made already by the earliest writing prophet Amos: "You only have I chosen of all the families of the earth; therefore I will punish you for all your sins" (Amos 3:2).

26. See, e.g., Obadiah and Ps 137.

27. This text illustrates the two aspects of the frequent expression "day of the LORD" in the prophets. Depending on one's relationship to Yahweh, in that eschatological period one experiences either curse or blessing. See further Helyer, *Yesterday*, 294–302.

28. An allusion to C. S. Lewis' masterpiece, *The Lion, the Witch, and the Wardrobe*, in which the great lion Aslan represents Jesus Christ.

7

Salvation Oracles for Israel

The storm clouds of fury will give way to the rainbow of divine grace and covenant recommitment.

—Daniel Block

You are my dear flock, the flock of my pasture, my human flock, And I am your God. Decree of God, the Master.

—Ezekiel 34:31 (*MSG*)

INTRODUCTION

At long last, good news for Israel.[1] Ezekiel prophesies a massive change in Israel's fortunes. This turnaround has nothing to do with Israel's efforts to reform herself and return to the

1. Block titles this section "Positive Messages of Hope for Israel: The Gospel According to Ezekiel" (*Ezekiel*, 2:268).

ancient homeland by her own efforts; it has everything to do with Yahweh's amazing grace taking the initiative in this remarkable transformation.

YAHWEH THE GOOD SHEPHERD OF ISRAEL (34:1–24)

Chapter 34 consists of two oracles, a judgment oracle upon the false shepherds of Israel (34:1–10), and a judgment-salvation oracle concerning the sheep of Israel (34:11–24).

The false shepherds are easily recognized as the faithless kings of Israel who plundered the flock and lived off what they produced. Jeremiah has a similar woe oracle against the derelict kings who destroyed and scattered the sheep of Israel (Jer 34:1–4). The primary indictment against the shepherds is their failure to strengthen the weak, heal the sick, and bind up the wounded. In short, they haven't taken care of the flock, only themselves.[2] Yahweh the divine judge sentences the derelicts for failing to fulfill covenant obligations as shepherds over Israel: "I am against the shepherds and will hold them accountable for my flock. I will remove them from tending the flock so that the shepherds can no longer feed themselves" (Ezek 34:10). That's the bad news; the good news follows: "I will rescue my flock from their mouths, and it will no longer be food for them" (34:10). A remarkable salvation oracle follows. Yahweh the Good Shepherd steps into Israel's story at its all-time low and sets in motion five distinct saving acts culminating in an all-time high.

He must first search for his scattered sheep. What is interesting is that he must rescue them "from all the places where they have been scattered" (34:12), namely, "the nations" and "countries" where they were scattered "on a day of clouds and darkness" (34:13). This is expansive language for the region where Israel had been exiled in the eighth and seventh centuries BC. The deportation of the northern tribes following the destruction of Samaria

2. This indictment echoes what Jeremiah said about Jehoiakim and his successor Jehoiachin (Jer 22:13–30).

in 722 BC was primarily to northern Syria. The Judean deportees were resettled along the Tigris-Euphrates Rivers in Iraq. One gets the impression, however, that the scattering mentioned by Ezekiel was much more extensive. In fact, all three major prophets describe a worldwide dispersion necessitating an equally worldwide recovery operation.[3] All of that to say, the language used by Ezekiel implies what history confirms, namely, a truly worldwide Jewish diaspora spanning the globe.

Yahweh then regathers his dispersed people from the nations of the world to their ancient homeland, the despoiled and deserted mountains of Israel (34:13). In chapter 36, the prophet reverses the judgment oracle against the mountains of Israel in chapter 6—the two chapters thus functioning like bookends. In the former, the mountains become deserted; in the latter, they "will produce branches and fruit for my people Israel, for they will soon come home" (36:8). The Sovereign LORD promises: "I will settle people on you as in the past and will make you prosper more than before" (36:11). And once again, the mountains "are alive with the sound of music."[4]

Yahweh must first attend to a matter of grave importance—there are impostors in the flock who return to the land. These gatecrashers must be culled from the flock. This is just another reminder in Scripture that mere profession is inadequate; genuine commitment is a prerequisite for feeding in the green pastures and drinking from the still waters (Ps 23). The pretenders trample the grass and muddle the waters by shoving, butting, and driving away the true sheep. Yahweh's sheep, on the other hand, are described as lean and weak.[5] This is a telling insight into the nature of those who are saved. As Paul pointedly reminds the Corinthians, "God chose the foolish things of the world to shame the wise; God chose the weak things of the world to shame the strong. God chose the lowly things of this world and the despised things—and the things that are not—to nullify the things that are, so that no one may

3. See Isa 11:12; Jer 31:8.

4. Adapted from the musical *The Sound of Music* (1965).

5. KJV has "sick" for "weak." The Hebrew term conveys both ideas.

boast before him. It is because of him that you are in Christ Jesus" (1 Cor 1:27–30).

The fat sheep are put on guard: "I will judge between one sheep and another" (Ezek 34:22). With this Paul is in complete accord: "For we must all appear before the judgment seat of Christ, so that each of us may receive what is due us for the things done while in the body, whether good or bad" (2 Cor 5:10). Those who pretend to be true believers but by their actions destroy God's temple must face this reality: "God will destroy that person, for God's temple is sacred, and you together are that temple" (1 Cor 3:17). Pretenders will hear this dreadful sentence from the Master: "I never knew you. Away from me, you evildoers" (Matt 7:23). The punishment is terrible indeed: "Then they will go away to eternal punishment" (Matt 25:46).

The returned sheep no longer suffer under rapacious shepherds. "I will place over them one shepherd, my servant David, and he will tend them and be their shepherd. I the LORD will be their God, and my servant David will be prince among them" (34:23–24). A majority of Christian interpreters understand "my servant David" to be the Messiah descended from David and fulfilling Yahweh's promise: "Your house and your kingdom will endure forever before me; your throne will be established forever" (2 Sam 7:16). Peter's Pentecost sermon proclaims precisely this point: "God promised him [David] on oath that he would place one of his descendants on his throne" (Acts 2:30).[6] A minority view holds that David himself will be raised up from the dead and assume his place on the throne of Israel.[7]

6. Cf. John 7:42; Rom 1:3; Acts 13:22; 2 Tim 2:8; Rev 5:5; 22:16.

7. "Nothing in Ezekiel 34:23 *demands* that Ezekiel was not referring to the literal King David who will be resurrected to serve as Israel's righteous prince. David is referred to by name elsewhere in passages that look to the future restoration of Israel (cf. Jer. 30:9; Ezek. 37:24–25; Hosea 3:5). Also Ezekiel indicated that David will be the prince (*nāśî'*) of the restored people (Ezek. 34:24; 37:25). This same 'prince' will then offer sin offerings for himself during the millennial period (45:22; 46:4). Such actions would hardly be appropriate for the sinless Son of God, but they would be for David. So it seems this is a literal reference to a resurrected David. In place of the false shepherds God will resurrect a true shepherd to tend his sheep" (Dyer, *Ezekiel*, 1:1296).

In either case, Ezekiel's prophecy looks beyond this age and glimpses the millennial kingdom during which time God's covenant promises to Israel are fulfilled and "the Israelites will return and seek the LORD their God and David their King" (Hos 3:5).[8] Jeremiah, Ezekiel's fellow prophet and contemporary, strikes the same note: "they will serve the LORD their God and David their king, whom I will raise up for them" (Jer 30:9). In short, Yahweh restores his people as one nation under the leadership of the Good Shepherd (John 10:11, 14), the descendant of David whom Christians confess as the Lord Jesus Christ.

In addition, Yahweh establishes a covenant of peace with his people Israel entailing safety from "savage beasts" (34:25) and "showers of blessing" (34:26). A safe and satisfied people at last acknowledge their savior. This covenant corresponds to Jeremiah's prophecy of a new covenant (Jer 31:31–37). Both prophets also call it "an everlasting covenant."[9]

Once again, we observe a remarkable agreement between these contemporaries ministering hundreds of miles apart. This congruence should not surprise us given the inspiration of the self-same Holy Spirit at work in each man—the conductor of the symphony we now call the Holy Scripture. The unity of Scripture is the end product. "For prophecy never had its origin in the human will, but prophets, though human, spoke from God as they were carried along by the Holy Spirit" (2 Pet 1:21).

JUDGMENT ORACLE AGAINST EDOM (35:1–15)

This judgment oracle against Edom seems out of place in the midst of restoration prophecies. Furthermore, a short judgment oracle against Edom already appears in the section devoted to oracles against the nations (25:12–14). So, why another, lengthier

8. "[T]hese promises were given to the house of Israel. Since only a few of the Jewish people were gathered to the Good Shepherd in His first appearing, there will come a day when the **house of Israel** will be regathered and God will again make with them His covenant of peace." (Hall, "Ezekiel," 460).

9. Jer 32:40; 33:20–21; 50:5; Ezek 16:60; 37:26.

judgment oracle inserted here? Perhaps the answer lies in Edom's long-standing animosity towards Israel, manifested by numerous atrocities.[10] For this reason Edom foreshadows the eschatological enemy Gog and Magog whose assault against the returned people of God in her homeland is narrated in chapters 38–39. Ezekiel's prophecy assures the reader that no enemy, however powerful, can reverse Yahweh's regathering and restoration of his covenant people. The final act of redemptive history unfolds according to plan.

VISION OF THE DRY BONES (37:1–14)

The prophet experiences another extraordinary vision. He is transported by the Spirit—this time to a valley "full of bones." With a light touch Wright says, "It was day-trip time again."[11] Almost certainly we should distinguish this vision from the visionary visit to Jerusalem in chapters 8–11. The Jerusalem visit involved observing things that were actually going on, although not in real time. This vision of the valley of dry bones is different; it's symbolic and represents something that will happen in real time although not in the form or manner in which the prophet perceives it. After unpacking the vision, I think my distinction will make better sense.

The vision unfolds in several stages. First, the prophet is placed in the middle of a valley littered with many dry bones. It was as if a vast army had been destroyed in a catastrophic battle and the corpses were left to rot until only bleached bones remained. Yahweh leads the prophet "back and forth among them" (37:2).[12]

After the magnitude of this mass graveyard sinks in, Yahweh then asks Ezekiel a leading question: "Son of man, can these bones

10. "Because you harbored an ancient hostility and delivered the Israelites over to the sword at the time of their calamity" (Ezek 35:5). See Amos 1:11–12; Obad 10–14.

11. Wright, *Ezekiel*, 303.

12. Wright draws attention to the particular discomfort such a scene would have caused Ezekiel the priest. Contact with a corpse or bone was the most defiling of all ritual impurities (*Ezekiel*, 303). See further, Helyer, *Yesterday*, 131.

live?" He doesn't directly answer: "Sovereign LORD, you alone know" (37:3). Ezekiel doesn't say no; in fact, he believes Yahweh *can* give life to the dry bones. After all, Yahweh calls into being that which is not and does whatever he wills. Like Job, Ezekiel has no doubt about his incomparable power. "I know that you can do all things; no purpose of yours can be thwarted" (Job 42:2; See also Gen 18:14; Jer 32:17). But in this case, Ezekiel isn't sure what Yahweh's intentions are.

Yahweh follows up by requiring Ezekiel to step up—demonstrate his faith in the miracle-working God. "Prophesy to the bones and say to them, 'Dry bones, hear the word of the LORD!'" (37:4). Humanly speaking, this is an exercise in futility, unless of course, you really do believe Yahweh can bring life to dead bones. Ezekiel prophesies as commanded: "Dry bones, hear the word of the LORD!" (37:4)

What happens next is one of the most macabre visions a prophet ever experienced. In a virtual "valley of the shadow of death" (Ps 23:4 NIV mg), a great rattling sound reverberates across the plain. The bones begin to bond in their proper places—I hear in my mind the lyrics of the song "Dem Bones" with its rollicking refrain, "Now shake dem skeleton bones!" And how dem skeleton bones did shake, dancing like Hasidim on the basin floor![13]

It doesn't stop there. The skeletons undergo a process of embodiment; first the tendons, then flesh (muscle, fat, and entrails), and finally skin. The dance now takes on an even more ghoulish character as corpses cavort across the landscape.

But "there was no breath in them" (37:8). This required one final word from Yahweh, which is forthcoming: "Prophesy to the breath" (37:9). The prophet summons the breath from the four winds who breathes into the lifeless corpses. Immediately and miraculously "they came to life and stood up on their feet—a vast army" (37:10). The breath who gives life is identified: "I will put my Spirit in you and you will live" (37:14). The Hebrew word *ruah*

13. The Hasidic movement is well-known for its exuberant dancing, especially at weddings.

carries the basic meanings "wind, breath, and spirit."[14] All three occur in this passage ("breath," vv. 9, 10; "winds" v. 9; and "Spirit" v. 14). The point is that only the Spirit (*ruah*) of God gives breath and life (*ruah*), whether to embryos in the womb (Ps 139:13–16) or even, in this case, corpses in a cemetery.

One hears echoes from the second creation narrative, the creation of the first man: "Then the LORD God formed a man from the dust of the ground and breathed into his nostrils the breath of life, and the man became a living being" (Gen 2:7). The Spirit of the LORD bestows life—even life to the dead. This is a God-thing—only he can do it.[15]

Meaning of the Vision

This visionary transformation—from dry bones having no hope to living beings standing on their feet—depicts, metaphorically, Israel's national restoration in which Yahweh opens the graves of his scattered people and brings them back to their ancestral homeland (37:12). After restoration, Yahweh then puts his Spirit in them and they come alive spiritually possessing a living hope. Recognizing this sequence is crucial: a return to the land is the *prelude* to regeneration. Only when back in their ancestral homeland does spiritual rebirth occur. Once again, this harmonizes with Jeremiah who prophesies the same sequence of saving events in Israel's restoration (Jer 30–31; 33). The post-exilic prophet Zechariah is also on the same page envisioning a return followed by regeneration, in fact, his prophecy strikes many of the same notes and themes as Ezekiel.[16]

But there is more to be said. In the larger context of redemptive history, Ezekiel's vision of the dry bones contributes to the

14. See Clines, *Dictionary*, 7:427–40.

15. "The God who made the world and everything in it is the Lord of heaven and earth, . . . he himself gives everyone life and breath and everything else" (Acts 17:24–25). The apostle Paul proclaimed this before Epicurean and Stoic philosophers at a meeting of the Areopagus in Athens.

16. See Zech 12–13.

development of personal eschatology. During the exilic and post-exilic eras, the notion of a personal, bodily resurrection comes to the fore as a major hope.[17] Although there are intimations of bodily resurrection in Job 19:26–27, Ps 16:9–11, and Isa 25:7–8, the doctrine fully emerges only in Dan 12:2–3: "Multitudes who sleep in the dust of the earth will awake: some to everlasting life, others to shame and everlasting contempt. Those who are wise will shine like the brightness of the heavens, and those who lead many to righteousness, like the stars for ever and ever." The fact that Ezekiel, the prophet of exile, depicts Israel's national restoration in terms of bodily resurrection adds momentum to the doctrine of personal resurrection in the age to come.

By the time of Jesus, the doctrine of personal, bodily resurrection was a fundamental teaching of the Pharisees. Jesus affirmed this truth (Matt 22:23–32; John 11:24–26) and it passed into early Christianity as a lynchpin of faith.[18] The apostle Paul highlights the significance of Jesus' resurrection for all believers: "[He] has destroyed death and has brought life and immortality to light through the gospel" (2 Tim 1:10).

ONE STICK, ONE NATION (37:15–28)

The vision of the dry bones is followed by one more symbolic act summarizing Ezekiel's prophecies in chapters 34–37. Yahweh instructs the prophet: "Son of man, take two sticks of wood, and write on it 'Belonging to Judah and the Israelites associated with him.' Then take another stick of wood and write on it, 'Belonging to Joseph (that is, to Ephraim) and all the Israelites associated with him.' Join them together so that they will become one in your hand" (Ezek 37:15–17).

Ezekiel must have carried this joined stick about the settlement because it attracted attention and prompted the inhabitants to ask what it meant. To this inquiry Ezekiel had a ready answer.

17. See further Helyer, *Yesterday*, 339–47.

18. See 1 Cor 15:1–7.

Here in summary is Yahweh's plan for the dispersed and dispirited people of Israel:

- He will regather them in their own land (v. 21)
- He will reunite them as one nation (v. 22)
- He will cleanse them from their idolatry (v. 23)
- He will place David as king over them (v. 24)
- He will make an everlasting covenant of peace with them (v. 26)
- He will dwell in their midst forever (v. 26)

The upshot of these actions culminates in universal recognition: "Then the nations will know that I the LORD make Israel holy, when my sanctuary is among them forever" (v. 28). The concluding note about the everlasting sanctuary anticipates Ezekiel's final vision in chapters 40–48. But before the finale comes a final crisis.

8

God Versus Gog

The destruction of Gog as the final great enemy of Israel and Yahweh thus stands as ultimate reassurance to God's people that their future is secure.

—Christopher J. H. Wright

INTRODUCTION

The dark night of exile is over. The dispersed people of Israel are regathered and restored to their ancient homeland. Yahweh cleanses them from all their impurities, gives them a new heart, and puts his Spirit in them. The Spirit "moves" them to follow his decrees and keep his laws (36:24–27). Their spiritual rebirth is now complete. They're not Jedis, they're something grander, because the Holy Spirit, not "the force," empowers them. The NT presents the same process of regeneration and sanctification demonstrating once again the unity of Scripture.

The land itself is transformed. "[The] land that was laid waste has become like the garden of Eden" (36:35) and the people will become "as numerous as sheep . . . and the cities filled with flocks of people" (36:38). Paradise on earth—an amazing turn of events!

But the mystery of evil once again raises its ugly head. Paradise is threatened by the primeval serpent. The Dark Lord, in a final, desperate act of rebellion, conjures up the most dangerous enemy ever to threaten the people of Israel. The last battle between God and Satan unfolds on the mountains of Israel.

No portion of Ezekiel's prophecy has attracted more attention from prophecy prognosticators than chapters 38–39. Interpretations proliferate with each new generation, with most winding up in the waste basket. Humility and restraint are required. What I offer below is an exposition of the essential message with no guarantees of certainty as to the specific details.

OUTLINE OF EVENTS (38:1—39:20)

Chapters 38 and 39 present two aspects of Gog's massive invasion of the land of Israel. Chapter 38 traces the events leading up to the invasion, the invasion itself, and Yahweh's decisive intervention and destruction of Gog's hordes. Chapter 39 describes the grim cleanup operation in the aftermath.

Lead Up to the Invasion

Yahweh commands Ezekiel to utter a judgment oracle against an evil empire, an ungodly alliance of nations under the leadership of Prince Gog. The oracle is not included in chapters 25–32, probably because it occurs during the end times of chapters 34–48.

But having said that, questions leap off the page. Who is Gog? Where is Magog? Where are Meshek and Tubal? Where are Gomer, Togarmah, and "the many nations"? What we can say is that included in the list are three known, historical nations, Persia, Cush, and Put, which suggests that the other names are also historical.

But who they are and where they are remains "a puzzlement."[1] "The honest answer is that nobody really knows, but not for want of trying."[2]

And when does this final battle occur? Should it be placed before the day of the LORD (i.e., during the great tribulation), at the end of that period, the sixth seal, the battle of Armageddon (Rev 16:12–16), or does it occur at the end of the millennial era? Each option has advocates. We find ourselves in the same quandary as the OT prophets: "Concerning this salvation, the prophets, who spoke of the grace that was to come to you, searched intently and with the greatest care, *trying to find out the time and circumstances* to which the Spirit of Christ in them was pointing when he predicted the sufferings of the Messiah and the glories that would follow" (1 Pet 1:10).

A word of caution: We go off the rails if we attempt a correlation of the biblical text with current world events. Unfortunately, this has been the default position for many expositors, ancient, medieval, and modern.[3] The result of this approach has proved

1. From the song "A Puzzlement," in the stage play *The King and I*. Lyrics by Oscar Hammerstein II.

2. "This question has been studied and discussed extensively. No satisfying conclusion has been reached, and the most popular solutions are questionable at best" (Richards, *Teachers' Commentary*, 507). What we can say is that Persia is modern Iran, Cush is Sudan, and Put is probably Libya. Most likely, Gomer refers to the Cimmerians and Beth Togarmah is ancient Armenia. According to Ezek 27:3, Meshech and Tubal were trading partners with Tyre and probably located in central and eastern Turkey. See further Yamauchi, *Foes*, 19–27.

3. "No one can doubt the popularity in our day of reading the Bible alongside the newspaper, looking for how God's message to Ezekiel, Daniel, and John (Revelation) is coming true in our lifetime. Books that 'unlock the secrets of the end times' sell millions of copies, and few evangelicals in America question the propriety of this approach." See https://www.ligonier.org/learn/devotionals/gog-and-magog/. See also Kelle, *Ezekiel*, 308, 321–24. Early church fathers identified Gog with Roman emperors. Ambrose from the early fifth century AD equated Gog with the invading Goths. In the twentieth century, it has been fashionable among Protestant fundamentalists to fasten on Russia. E.g., Hal Lindsey of *The Late Great Planet Earth* fame had a chapter entitled "Russia is a Gog." That book, by the way, has sold over fifteen million copies! He was not the first and certainly not the last in that tradition to hold to this view. It is still championed by Tim LaHaye and Pat Roberston among many

more embarrassing than enlightening. "Many . . . look for trends in international relationships that seem to them to portend increased hostility toward Israel on the part of Soviet Russia and the Arab nations. But it is always questionable to interpret current events with the fulfillment of Bible prophecy until *after* that fulfillment takes place. When what Ezekiel describes comes to pass, we will all be sure just what it is these chapters actually describe."[4]

Some have equated Gog with the famous Gyges of Lydia, located in western Turkey.[5] Other possibilities include a king named Gaga—not to be confused with Lady Gaga!—mentioned in the Amarna Letters of the fourteenth century BC and Gagi king of the city-state Sabhi. But none of these historical persons and places fit the eschatological setting of chapters 38–39.

A number of expositors from the nineteenth and twentieth centuries correlated Meshek with Moscow and Tubal with the Russian city of Tubolsk, especially after the Bolshevik Revolution of 1917 and the spread of worldwide Communism.[6] The fall of

---

others. Robertson raised eyebrows in March 2022 by announcing on "The 700 Club" that Vladimir Putin was simply following God's wishes and the invasion of Ukraine was a prelude to his attack upon Israel and the battle of Armageddon. These claims were supported by quoting passages from Ezek 38. (Bella, "Putin Compelled"). I once tuned in to the "The Hal Lindsey Report" in which he emphatically told his viewers that all that is needed to be a sound interpreter of prophecy is a Bible and a current newspaper. On the back cover of Lindsey's book, *There's a New World Coming*, the advertising blurb says, "This Book is more Up-to-Date than Tomorrow's Newspaper!" Such an approach bypasses the more demanding process of first understanding the text in its historical, cultural, and linguistic context, and then, even more challenging, engaging the hermeneutical question of its significance for today's reader.

4. Richards, *Bible Reader Companion*, 507. Note that Richards wrote this just before the Soviet Union collapsed. See also Rooker, *Ezekiel*, 602.

5. Gyges founded a dynasty in Lydia and reigned from ca. 687–652 BC, but he lived almost a century before Ezekiel.

6. *SRB* says in a footnote on Ezek 38:2: "That the primary reference is to the northern (European) powers, headed up by Russia all agree. . . . The reference to Meshech and Tubal (Moscow and Tobolsk is a clear mark of identification)" (883). Walter Chamberlain had already made this identification in 1854 (Lindsey, *Planet Earth*, 62). Both men were no doubt influenced by Wilhelm Gesenius' *Hebrew-Chaldee Lexicon to the Old Testament Scriptures* first published in 1809 with many subsequent revisions. But more than two

Communism in Russia in 1992 did little to dissuade advocates. Hal Lindsey, Tim LaHaye, Pat Robertson, and a host of others continue to champion an end-times invasion of coalition forces led by Russia sweeping down from the north, joined by armies from the east (Red China), west (Germany = Gomer and Beth Togarmah), and south (Islamic forces = Libya and Put).

A sounder approach takes seriously the fact that "every book in the Bible . . . has *historical particularity*; each document is conditioned by the language, time, and culture in which it was originally written."[7] Drawing on the work of scholars specializing in ancient history and languages provides a more informed understanding of the text.[8] While the identity of Gog remains uncertain and is probably a symbolic name, the places mentioned in the text can all be reasonably located on the fringes of the Mediterranean basin during the sixth century BC. These peoples lay "beyond the pale" of the surrounding nations against whom the prophet delivered judgment oracles (chs. 25–32). As such, they represent nations who reject the reality and witness of Yahweh the God of Israel.[9]

---

centuries of archaeological excavation, discovery, and scholarship have greatly expanded our knowledge of the biblical world. "All informed references and studies acknowledge that the association with Moscow and Tobolsk is untenable" (Yamauchi, *Foes*, 24–25).

7. Fee and Stuart, *How to Read*, 21. Stuart makes an emphatic point: "The communicator must help his or her audience to get beyond this misinterpretation (i.e., Meshech = Moscow; Tubal = Tobolsk; and Rosh = Russia], and a good starting place is one of the basic rules of interpreting Bible prophecy: no modern nation is mentioned in the Bible" (*Ezekiel*, 343).

8. This background material is accessible in commentaries, dictionaries, and encyclopedias. Digital software programs like Logos Bible Software place these resources literally at one's fingertips. To forgo such tools and rely on the Holy Spirit's illumination *alone* is inadequate for the task because the Holy Spirit doesn't somehow implant the necessary contextual background in one's mind. To quote a line from the Clint Eastwood movie *Pale Rider*: "the Spirit ain't worth spit without a little exercise." Biblical expositors first need to do the hard work of exegesis, then turn to the equally hard task of exposition, i.e., explaining its meaning for modern readers.

9. "Unlike the Egyptians, Assyrians, and Babylonians, with whom Judah had frequent contact, the peoples in the distant north were shrouded in mystery. The reports of these mysterious people groups that filtered down spoke of

Motivation for the Invasion

Why does Gog invade Israel? The short answer is wealth and strategic location, "living at the center of the [earth]" (38:16).[10] Furthermore, the loot is easy pickings because it is a "peaceful and unsuspecting people" (38:11).

Timing of the Invasion

So, *when* does this invasion occur? The description of peace and security hardly fits current realities, given the fact that the State of Israel is the strongest military power in the entire Middle East, maintains constant readiness and vigilance against any military threat, and is a major player in international arms sales. Furthermore, this massive invasion in chapters 38–39 follows hard on the heels of the drama of national restoration and spiritual rebirth depicted in chapters 34–37.

A popular option identifies Gog's invasion with the Battle of Armageddon in Rev 16:12–20. The beast or antichrist of Rev 13 is Gog and the temporal setting is just prior to the second coming of Christ, as depicted in Rev 19. The reference to Israel as "peaceful and unsuspecting" is the result of a seven-year covenant with Israel in which the antichrist guarantees their security for seven years but breaks it after three-and-a-half years (Dan 9:27) and invades the land. This scenario relies on too many assumptions and loose ends to be convincing.[11]

An important factor for determining the time period comes from Rev 20:7–10, which places Gog's invasion at the end of

---

wild people, brutal, and barbaric. This combination of mystery and brutality made Gog and his confederates perfect symbols of the archetypal enemy, rising against God and his people" (Block, *Ezekiel*, 2:436).

10. I think *haaretz* should be translated "earth," as in NRSV and ESV or "world" as in HCSB.

11. For an evaluation of the various temporal options, see Alexander, "Fresh Look," 155–69. He appeals to the concept of multiple fulfillments whereby Gog is both the beast in Rev 19 and then represents the rebellious nations of Rev 20.

Christ's millennial reign on earth. Satan is released from the Abyss and permitted a final, futile attempt to overthrow God's kingdom on earth. Following his standard mode of operation, he deceives the nations in the four corners of the earth—symbolized as Gog and Magog—and gathers them for an assault on "the camp of God's people, the city he loves," that is, Jerusalem. This post-millennial setting, though not without problems, best fits Ezekiel's prophecy against Gog.

Outcome of the Invasion

When Gog's hordes threaten redeemed Israel, Yahweh rises up like a warrior and joins battle against his foes. "My hot anger will be aroused" (38:18).[12] Wright compares this description of Yahweh to "cartoon-strip scenarios."[13] Just like the Incredible Hulk, you don't want to make Yahweh angry![14] A torrent of rain, hailstones, and burning sulfur batter Gog's goons. In an awesome display of Yahweh's "greatness and holiness" (39:23), the fertile mountains of Israel become a vast, killing field—strewn with countless, charred corpses. Gog is gone for good.

Aftermath of the Invasion

A massive cleanup operation lasts for seven years. The first seven months are taken up with burying the corpses, lest the mountains of Israel become a stench and ritually unclean. Yahweh also summons his sanitation corps, "every kind of bird and all the wild animals" (Ezek 39:17), for a grisly banquet of carrion.[15] A huge

12. See Longman and Reid, *God Is a Warrior*.

13. Wright, *Ezekiel*, 317.

14. This is a reference to the 1978 TV series *The Incredible Hulk* in which Dr. David Banner, when angered, morphs into a creature of incredible strength. The character was based on a Marvel Comics character, the Hulk, and made into a Hollywood film in 2008.

15. In the Apocalypse birds are summoned to a similar banquet of flesh in the aftermath of the great battle against the beast (antichrist) and his minions (Rev 19:17–18).

national cemetery, Hamon Gog, is set aside to commemorate Yahweh's victory over Gog.[16] After seven months of the cleanup operation, search teams are deployed to mark the site of any remaining human bones so they can be interred in Hamon Gog.

Theology of the Invasion

Several times the reader is informed why this climactic battle, "a memorable day" for the people of God (39:13), must take place. In short, Gog invades God's land in order that "the nations may know me when I am proved holy through you [Gog] before their eyes" (38:16), a theme repeated throughout this section.[17] But even more importantly, "from that day forward the people of Israel will know that I am the Lord their God" (39:22).

Though counterintuitive, a comforting theological truth emerges from Gog's invasion of the land of Israel. With conceited confidence, Gog "will advance against [Yahweh's] people Israel like a cloud that covers the land" (38:22). But just when it appears that he will crush Israel, Yahweh enters the fray and strikes back: "I will execute judgment on [Gog] with plague and bloodshed; . . . pour down torrents of rain, hailstones and burning sulfur on him and on his troops and on the many nations with him" (38:22). Redemptive history resonates with this affirmation: Yahweh is the great defender and protector of his people. The Psalmist appeals to the great champion of Israel: "Contend, O Lord, with those who contend with me; fight against those who fight against me. Take up shield and buckler; arise and come to my aid. Brandish spear and

16. The exact location is unclear, but the description fits the Jezreel Valley, "the only valley that runs in an east-west direction" (Rooker, *Ezekiel*, 603).

17. Ezek 38:23; 39:6, 7, 21–23, 27–29. After the crossing of the Jordan River, Joshua testifies to his fellow countrymen: "He did this so that all the peoples of the earth might know that the hand of the Lord is powerful and so that you might always fear the Lord your God" (Jos 4:23). Ezekiel makes precisely the same point.

javelin against those who pursue me. Say to my soul, 'I am your salvation'" (Ps 35:1–3).

Readers familiar with C. S. Lewis' book *The Lion, the Witch and the Wardrobe* will recall that the great lion Aslan represents Jesus Christ. Just when it seemed the army of Narnia under Kings Peter and Edmund and Queens Susan and Lucy was about to be overwhelmed by the Wicked Witch Jadis (symbolizing Satan) and her army of demons, Aslan leaps into the fray, binding her and consigning her to prison. Lewis' masterpiece draws upon the imagery of the book of Revelation, which in turn is indebted to Ezekiel.[18]

The Dark Lord and the powers of darkness assail and may even defeat God's people for a season, but in the end, "the gates of Hades will not overcome it [my church]" (Matt 16:19).[19] Pastor John of Patmos had a vision similar to that of Ezekiel in which "the beast and the kings of the earth and their armies gathered together to wage war against the rider on the horse [whose name is King of kings, and Lord of lords (Rev. 19:16)] and his army. But the beast was captured, and with it the false prophet. . . . The two of them were thrown alive into the fiery lake of burning sulfur" (Rev 19:19–20). No one can stand against the Lord God Almighty, not even the incredible beast![20]

18. Cf. Rev 19:19–21 with Ezek 38:19–23.

19. The notion that Yahweh is a warrior who fights for his people ties the Testaments together. The idea first explicitly appears in the song of the sea sung after Israel escapes Pharaoh's army by passing through the Red Sea. "The LORD is a warrior; The LORD is his name. Pharaoh's chariots and his army he has hurled into the sea. . . . Your right hand, LORD, shattered the enemy" (Exod 15:3, 6). It last appears in the Apocalypse: "The armies of heaven were following him [Christ]. . . . Coming out of his mouth is a sharp sword with which to strike down the nations. He will rule them with an iron scepter. He treads the winepress of the fury of the wrath of God Almighty" (Rev 19:13–15). For a full treatment see Longman and Reid, *God Is a Warrior*.

20. "Who is like the beast? Who can wage war against it?" (Rev 13:4)

SUMMARY OF EZEKIEL'S NIGHT VISIONS (39:21–29)

In 39:21–29 we have a succinct summary of Yahweh's redemption of his people Israel, providing answers to some troubling questions. Why did Yahweh punish Israel so severely for her many sins? And why did he then have compassion on them, forget all their unfaithfulness, restore them to their land, and cleanse them from their filth? The answer is clear: "I will display my glory" (39:21). The Westminster Shorter Catechism captures this truth in its first question. What is the chief end of man? The answer: "Man's chief end is to glorify God, and to enjoy him forever."[21] God's glory comes into focus when the people of God know that he is the Lord their God. And this is true also for the nations. Once again, the supreme importance of knowing God shines through. No wonder this theme of knowing God runs all through the prophets. Isaiah laments the deplorable situation in his day: "Israel does not know, my people do not understand" (Isa 1:3).

The six night-time oracle-visions are capped off in chapters 40–48 with a seventh, climactic visionary experience in which, once again, Ezekiel visits the city of Jerusalem. This time, however, a dramatically different city comes into view, a city adorned with a gleaming new temple, undefiled by degrading idolatry and radiating with Yahweh's glory.

21. *Westminster Shorter Catechism*, Q.1.

9

Yahweh's Glory Returns

Mine eyes have seen the glory of the coming of the Lord.

—*Battle Hymn of the Republic*

The dark days of divine abandonment are over. The king has come home.

—Christopher J. H. Wright

INTRODUCTION (40:1—48:35)

Ezekiel structures his prophecy like a row of books bounded by bookends. Beginning with a blazing vision of Yahweh's throne-chariot in chapter 1, it ends with a brilliant vision of a new temple in chapters 40–48. What surprised Ezekiel in the first vision along the Kebar River was the unexpected reality that the holy Lord was there—in a pagan land no less. He concludes his book, after going on a guided, virtual reality tour of the new temple, with this bookend: "And the name of the city from that time on will be: THE LORD IS THERE" (48:35).

But there is another set of bookends, equally significant for understanding Ezekiel's message. The two bookends are the two visionary visits to Jerusalem, so dramatically different in content and outcome. The first, in chapters 8–11, describes the appalling spiritual condition of contemporary Jerusalem's priests and people, resulting in the departure of Yahweh's glory from the temple in chapter 10. The second, in chapters 40–48, describes a new temple served by a restored priesthood and accessible to a reconciled people having "an undivided heart" [and] "a new spirit in them" (11:19). To this new temple the glory of Yahweh returns and resides forever (43:1–12). A perfect conclusion to "the gospel according to Ezekiel."

It must be admitted, however, that in chapters 40–48 one must persevere through a mass of details. Dimensions and features of the new temple are meticulously measured and recorded. I spare the reader an exposition of the minutiae and instead reflect on three fundamental questions.

1. Why was Ezekiel required to record in such detail the dimensions and regulations of the new temple?
2. When, if ever, will Ezekiel's temple be built?
3. What is the theological meaning of the new temple?

JERUSALEM REIMAGED

April 28, 573 BC, the twenty-fifth year after Ezekiel's exile, the twentieth year after Ezekiel's first visionary visit to Jerusalem, and the fourteenth year after the fall of the city in 587 BC, the hand of Yahweh transported the prophet back to the Holy City. But what a dramatic difference! The first visit unnerved the prophet: he saw terrible things.[1] "Alas, Sovereign LORD! Will you completely

1. Several years ago, I saw a billboard in Atlanta advertising the business of a certain plumber. The sign said it all: "We've seen terrible things!"

destroy the remnant of Israel?" (11:13). But now Yahweh placed Ezekiel on a high mountain and he saw glorious things.[2] On the south side of the mountain, the prophet saw "some buildings that looked like a city" (40:2). As it turns out, these buildings belonged to a massive temple complex.

This mountaintop experience echoes that of Moses on Mount Sinai. Like his predecessor, Ezekiel delivers detailed legislation for the performance of priestly duties.[3] And, like Moses, Ezekiel receives a detailed description of a dwelling place for Yahweh—the former being the wilderness tabernacle, the latter, the glorious new temple on Mount Zion.[4] There is another striking parallel in that both Moses and Ezekiel survey the promised land from atop a mountain: Moses from Mount Nebo (Deut 32:48–52) and Ezekiel from Mount Zion. Both experiences anticipate the apostle John's climactic vision of redemptive history in which he was "carried . . . away in the Spirit to a mountain great and high" (Rev 21:9) and saw "the Holy City, Jerusalem, coming down out of heaven from God" (Rev 21:10).

Ezekiel's tour of the new temple dominates the rest of his vision.[5] His tour is not self-guided—an angelic guide meets him at the gateway with "a linen cord and a measuring rod" (40:3) and conducts him throughout the temple precincts.[6] The city of Jerusalem itself gets scant attention—the prophet mentions only that each of its four sides was 4,500 cubits (ca. 1½ miles) and that this four-square city had twelve gates named after the twelve tribes of Israel (48:1–35). Our priest is totally taken up with the

2. November 26, 1922, archaeologist Howard Carter peered through a crack into Tutankhamun's undisturbed tomb and Lord Carnarvon asked him: "Can you see anything"? Carter replied, "Yes, I see wonderful things"!

3. Ezek 43:18—46:24.

4. Though Ezekiel's plan is lacking important measurements, such as height of walls.

5. For a virtual tour of the reconstructed temple see "Ezekiel Temple Vision (2012)" at https://bibliaprints.com/free-bible-animations/. See also the segments on chapters 41–43.

6. Ezekiel's angelic guide becomes a standard feature of Second Temple apocalyptic literature. See further, Helyer, *Exploring Jewish Literature*, 112–46.

magnificent structure to which the glory of Yahweh returns. We can scarcely blame him for his laser-like focus. This is his world and he revels in it.

METICULOUS METRICS

So why was it so important that measurements be accurately recorded? There must be more to it than Ezekiel having OCD! The Lord tells Ezekiel that he is to "tell the people of Israel everything you see" (40:4). But why? The answer is pastoral: "that they may be ashamed of their sins" (43:10). The argument seems to be that reflecting on the perfection of the temple produces a deep sense of shame and guilt—how horribly they defiled and dishonored the Holy One of Israel and his holy temple! But how graciously the Holy God of Israel prepares a perfect place in which to dwell with his restored people![7] Like the prodigal son who was overwhelmed by the waiting father's unexpected grace, so the returnees, reflecting on God's amazing grace, are not chastised for failure but challenged "to be faithful" (v. 11). The past is forgiven and forgotten.

VARIATIONS ON A THEME

That brings us to the vexed question of fulfillment. Should this section be interpreted literally, figuratively, or a combination of both? When, if ever, will this temple be built and will it literally conform to the careful measurements recorded by Ezekiel? Opinions sharply differ.[8] The answer to the question depends on one's hermeneutical approach, which in turn is greatly influenced by

7. One thinks of Jesus' parting words to his disciples: "My Father's house has many rooms. If that were not so, would I have told you that I am going there to prepare a place for you? And if I go and prepare a place for you, I will come back and take you to be with me that you also may be where I am" (John 14:2–4).

8. "The concluding chapters of Ezekiel form a kind of continental divide in the area of biblical interpretation" (Feinberg, *Ezekiel*, 233).

one's understanding of ecclesiology (doctrine of the church) and eschatology (doctrine of last things).[9]

Literal Approach

Dispensationalists believe Ezekiel's temple vision will be literally fulfilled during the millennial kingdom.[10] This even includes an active priesthood offering animal sacrifices, albeit as memorials rather than as atoning sacrifices. In support, appeal is made to the principle that literal interpretation should be adhered to unless the text itself points to a non-literal or figurative sense. In the case of Ezekiel's new temple vision, so it is argued, there are no such indicators to justify resorting to a non-literal interpretation, since it accords with the accounts of the building of the wilderness tabernacle and Solomon's temple. Furthermore, a literal interpretation is consonant with many other OT prophecies that were literally fulfilled.[11]

Of utmost importance in a dispensational approach is distinguishing between Israel and the church. In their view, Ezek 40–48 applies to the nation of Israel during the millennial kingdom, not to the church, and to interpret these chapters as symbolically or spiritually fulfilled in the church age introduces confusion. Dispensationalists teach that during the millennium Ezekiel's temple will be built according to the revealed specifications. The Hebrew prophetic promises of a golden age on earth will be literally fulfilled,

9. Hermeneutics is, in a general sense, the art of interpretation, but in biblical scholarship is often used in a more specific sense of discovering the meaning or significance of a text in the present. For further discussion of this point see Fee and Stuart, *How to Read*, 23–31.

10. For an overview of the various millennial options, see Grenz, *Millennial Maze*. For a brief summary of the tenets of dispensationalism, see Rowdon, "Dispensational Theology," 200. For a more complete presentation of this approach see Ryrie, *Dispensationalism Today*.

11. E.g., the many prophecies of judgment on Israel and Judah, the exile and return, the birthplace and lineage of the Messiah, as well as his vicarious death and resurrection.

including the crown jewel of Jerusalem, the glorious temple, complete with restored priesthood and sacrifices.[12]

Virtually all dispensationalists and many premillennialists hold that before or during the great tribulation, a third temple, though not conforming to Ezekiel's blueprint, will be constructed on Mount Moriah, displacing the Islamic Dome of the Rock.[13] At the midpoint of the tribulation period (three-and-a-half years), the antichrist sets up an image of himself and demands that he be worshiped as God.[14]

Currently, the Temple Institute in Jerusalem, an organization of religious Jews in the orthodox tradition, is zealously making plans for rebuilding a third temple. The reader should be aware that this doesn't represent the official position of the Israeli government. The State of Israel strives to uphold the status quo with respect to the holy places and the communities who have jurisdiction over them. The Islamic Waqf oversees religious matters on the Haram esh Shariff ("the Noble Sanctuary").[15] Any attempt to rebuild the temple on this revered site would engulf the entire region in a holy war.[16]

Most of those in the Reformed tradition interpret the vision spiritually or symbolically.[17] In their view, "we are dealing

12. See Isa 2:1–5; Zech 14:16–21.

13. A few argue for a different location for the original temple—either just to the north or just to the south of the present-day Dome of the Rock. In which case, a supposed third temple could be built without destroying the Noble Sanctuary. In the opinion of a majority of professional archaeologists and historians, the arguments for these alternative sites are groundless. See Ritmeyer and Ritmeyer, *Secrets*, 57–89.

14. See Mark 13:14–19 ; Matt 24:15–21; 2 Thess 2:4; Rev 11:1–2.

15. This is the Arabic designation for the site Jews call the Temple Mount.

16. In my opinion, it is ill-advised for Christians to get on board with attempts to build the third temple. Such a temple, if realized, has no future in Christian eschatology; indeed, it seems destined to suffer desecration as did the first and second temples. See Dan 9:24–27; 11:31; 12:11; Matt 24:15; 2 Thess 2:3–4.

17. Those in the Reformed tradition are predominantly amillennial, i.e., no literal thousand-year reign of Christ and his saints on the earth after the second coming. The millennium is essentially a figurative way of describing

with theological geography rather than literal geography."[18] This approach insists that the NT people of God, both corporately and individually, constitute a new spiritual temple of God. The millennium is not a *literal* thousand-year reign of Christ and his saints on the earth following the great tribulation and preceding the eternal state; rather, it symbolizes the *present reign of Christ* in his people, both individually and corporately. In general, Reformed theology insists that Ezekiel's temple vision be interpreted from the vantage point of the NT perspective.

A third approach steers a middle course in which the fulfillment, understood in spiritual or symbolic terms, occurs during a future, millennial age on earth.[19] Ezekiel thus envisions ideal worship through the lens of his own time; namely, a rebuilt Jerusalem temple and a reinstituted Zadokite priesthood. This is analogous to the account of Gog's invasion of Israel in the latter days in which the weaponry employed is appropriate to Ezekiel's day, not our own—after all, it had to make sense to the original readers.[20] In short, the Christian reader must distinguish between what the vision meant to Ezekiel and his audience and what it now means to us.[21]

---

the present reign of Christ in his church. There are some Reformed theologians who are premillennialists and also adhere to covenant theology. For a brief overview of the history and beliefs of Reformed theology, see Letham, "Reformed Theology," 569–72.

18. Duguid, *Ezekiel*, loc. 9657.

19. As argued by Ellison, *Ezekiel*, 137–44.

20. Tim LaHaye and Hal Lindsey interpret the passage as referring to modern weapons. They insist, however, that Ezekiel's description of the future Jerusalem temple and its priestly cult must be taken literally. The problem is you can't have your cake and eat it too!

21. An important principle of scriptural interpretation takes seriously the cultural conditioning of the biblical text. See Fee and Stuart, *How to Read*, 23–31

Personal Reflections

I think it helpful to seek common ground. Almost all Christian interpreters agree that chapters 40–48 are in some sense messianic and that no such temple has yet been built. The temple of Zerubbabel and Joshua in the sixth century BC fell far short of the dimensions and grandeur of Solomon's Temple; nor should they be faulted for this, because the returnees lacked the resources and manpower to carry out such an ambitious project. According to the book of Ezra, the "older priests and Levites and family heads, who had seen the former temple, wept aloud when they saw the foundation of this temple being laid" (Ezra 3:12). The prophet Haggai, a contemporary of Ezra, explains why. "How does it look to you now? Does it not seem to you like nothing?" (Hag 2:3). But at least it was something.

The Hasmoneans enlarged the Temple Mount area to the south but it was Herod the Great who doubled its size.[22] His engineers leveled off the entire Temple Mount and built massive retaining walls providing a spacious platform for surrounding colonnades and courtyards. The sanctuary itself, sheathed in marble and gilded with gold, was one of the wonders of the world in the first century AD. Josephus (a Jewish historian roughly contemporary with the apostle Paul) waxes eloquent in his description: "Viewed from without, the Sanctuary had everything that could amaze either mind or eyes. Overlaid all round with stout plates of gold, the first rays of the sun it reflected so fierce a blaze of fire that those who endeavored to look at it were forced to turn away as if they had looked straight at the sun. To strangers as they approached it seemed in the distance like a mountain covered with snow; for any part not covered with gold was dazzling white."[23] Jesus' disciples were indeed dazzled: "Look, Teacher! What massive

22. The Hasmonean family are better known as the Maccabees. Simon the Maccabee extended the Temple Mount to the south in 142 BC. Herod's project began in ca. 19 BC and was not completely finished when the Jewish Revolt broke out in AD 66 leading to its destruction in AD 70. The Temple Mount (Haram esh-Sharif) consists of about thirty-seven acres.

23. Josephus, *Jewish War*, 304.

stones! What magnificent buildings!" (Mark 13:1). The later rabbis exclaimed: "He who has not seen Herod's building, has never in his life seen a truly grand building."[24] But here's the problem: Ezekiel's temple, if built according to his measurements, would dwarf even Herod's magnificent structure and require a massive topographical transformation.

"Did Ezekiel, then, think of his temple in a literal way as something that would one day be built to the specifications of his vision?"[25] Wright answers his own question: "There can be little doubt that he did indeed expect that the temple would be rebuilt in Jerusalem."[26] He goes on, however, to argue that what the text meant to *Ezekiel* is not necessarily what it means for *us* today.[27]

Those who insist on a literal approach push back against this distinction and cite evidence from this specific text and from other OT texts in support of their contention. For example, in 43:10–12, someone inside the temple—and since the glory of Yahweh had just entered the temple, it must have been Yahweh himself—speaks to the prophet: "Write these things down before them so that they may be faithful to its design and follow all its regulations" (43:11). One could argue that just as Moses built the tabernacle following a divinely revealed blueprint on Mount Sinai and Solomon built the first temple according to the blueprint provided by King David, so too Ezekiel's temple will be built according to the measurements of the "man whose appearance was like bronze" (40:3).

On the other hand, does 43:10–12 *legislate* the building of this temple? What the prophet says is that the people should be "faithful to its design." Sometimes overlooked is the observation that Ezekiel describes *in a vision* a temple *that already exists*. Nowhere does he say the returned remnant should *build* anything. In

24. *B. Bat.* 4a.

25. Wright, *Ezekiel*, 338.

26. Wright, *Ezekiel*, 338.

27. Wright, *Ezekiel*, 338–43. On the important distinction between what a text *meant* and what it now *means*, see Fee and Stuart, *How to Read*, 29–31, 71–74.

other words, this visionary temple is a perfect place for a perfected people to offer up perfect worship.[28]

Here is another weighty objection against a literal fulfillment: "There are things . . . so improbable physically as to preclude a purely literal interpretation. . . . The square of the temple . . . is six times as large as the circuit of the wall enclosing the old temple, and larger than all the earthly Jerusalem."[29] The geological transformation required to accommodate the temple, its city, and its environs would be *massive*—but there is no mention in the text of such a phenomenon.[30]

A further feature militates against literal fulfillment. The life-giving water proceeding from the threshold of the temple and flowing into the Dead Sea increases in volume exponentially without any tributaries! This unparalleled physical phenomenon could, of course, be attributed to supernatural causes, but such an ad hoc appeal to divine intervention runs counter to the rest of Ezekiel's straightforward description.[31] That the living water also appears in poetic texts in the OT and is spiritually interpreted in NT texts strengthens the objection.[32]

Given that Ezekiel, in a visionary state, sees an already existing temple and nowhere urges his fellow Judeans to build it following the revealed specifications, a completely literal approach fails to do justice to its significance for today.

28. See further Kelle, *Ezekiel*, 329.

29. Jamison et al., *Ezekiel*, 357. Block agrees: "All in all Ezekiel's scheme appears highly contrived, casting doubt on any interpretation that expects a literal fulfillment of his plan" (*Ezekiel*, 2:502).

30. To be sure, the post-exilic prophet Zechariah does speak of Yahweh standing on the Mount of Olives and the mount being split in two forming a valley to enable escape from Jerusalem (Zech 14:4).

31. Feinberg justifies the injection of the supernatural: "The chapters do not pretend to describe natural, but rather supernatural, conditions" (*Ezekiel*, 238). But, in reply, with the exception of the river (47:1–12), the chapters don't pretend to describe supernatural conditions at all.

32. For the OT see Ps. 36:8–9; 46:9; Joel 3:18; Zech 13:1; 14:8. For the NT see John 4:10; 7:37–38; Rev 7:17; 21:6; 22:1–2.

Here, it seems to me, lies the theological meaning of Ezekiel's temple vision: the idealized temple anticipates God's ideal future for his redeemed people. As such, it functions as a message of hope for the "depressing realities of captivity in Ezekiel's day."[33] But it also looks well beyond the exile into the eschatological blessings projected for the redeemed people of God. The NT teaches that *already* the church of Jesus Christ is living in the last days and *now* constitutes a spiritual temple in which God himself dwells. When Jesus told the Jews that if they destroyed the temple, he would raise it again in three days, John inserts this editorial comment: "But the temple he had spoken of was his body" (John 2:21). Later, in the upper room discourse, John adds this saying of Jesus: "Anyone who loves me will obey my teaching. My Father will love them, and we will come to them and make our home with them" (John 14:23; cf. 17:20). In their pastoral letters, Paul and Peter further develop the teaching of Christ's church as the body of Christ and the temple of God.[34]

But what about the *not yet* dimension of the temple? Will there be a physical temple in the new Jerusalem? Pastor John of Patmos concludes the Apocalypse with this surprising announcement: "I did not see a temple in the city, because the Lord God Almighty and the Lamb are its temple" (Rev 21:22). In short, there is no need—it has served its purpose. Redemptive history comes full circle and the redeemed return to the primeval proximity to God enjoyed by our first parents (Gen 3:8). In fact, the new Jerusalem transcends the Edenic experience with unprecedented intimacy: "Look! God's dwelling place is now among the people, and he will dwell with them. They will be his people, and God himself will be with them and be their God" (Rev 21:3).

Divine closeness is enabled by a divine makeover. "The Lord Jesus Christ, who, by the power that enables him to bring everything under his control, will transform our lowly bodies so that

33. Stuart, *Ezekiel*, 357.

34. 1 Cor 3:16 (corporate); 1 Cor 6:19 (individual); Eph 2:20–22; 1 Pet 2:4–10 (corporate). See also 1 Cor 12:27; Eph 1:22–23; Col 1:18.

they will be like his glorious body" (Phil 3:20–21).[35] Glorified saints attain to what the medieval saints called the beatific vision, the ultimate experience of direct communication with God. "They will see his face, and his name will be on their foreheads" (Rev 22:4). Like a board game, after many trials and tribulations, the saints arrive home, safe, sound, and sanctified. This is the ultimate meaning of Ezekiel's vision.

THE RETURN OF YAHWEH'S GLORY (43:1–12)

Ezekiel's first visionary visit to Jerusalem was an Ichabod experience, "the Glory has departed from Israel" (1 Sam 4:21), but his second visionary visit was a *kabod* experience, "the glory of the LORD filled the temple" (Ezek 43:5).[36]

Chapters 40–48 narrate two movements in opposite directions: a *coming to* the temple and a *going from* the temple. The first narrates the return of Yahweh's glory from the east and its permanent residence in the Holy of Holies.[37] The second describes living water proceeding from under the temple threshold and coursing eastward down to the Dead Sea. Beginning as a mere trickle, it incrementally increases in volume until becoming an uncrossable river. Another amazing feature of the river is its vivifying capability. Along its banks great numbers of trees grow and once it arrives at the Dead Sea, it transforms the salty water into fresh—fish now thrive in its sweet waters.[38] Life-giving water from the temple totally transforms an arid wasteland into a veritable garden of Eden.

35. The Pauline letters affirm the same salvific outcome: See 1 Cor 15:52–57; 2 Cor 5:1–4; Rom 8:28–30. In connection with Ps 149:4, Purkiser observes that "salvation in its full biblical meaning is 'a beauty treatment' for the character, if not for the face and figure" (*Psalms*, 447).

36. Ichabod means literally "no glory."

37. This recalls the completion of the wilderness tabernacle in Moses' day ("Then the cloud covered the tent of meeting and the glory of the LORD filled the tabernacle" [Exod 40:34]) and the installation of the ark of the covenant in Solomon's new temple ("the glory of the LORD filled his temple" [1 Kgs 8:11]).

38. This is a huge transformation in that the water of the Salt Sea or Dead Sea is ten times more saline than ocean water.

A psalmist exclaims: "How priceless is your unfailing love, O God! . . . [Y]ou give them drink from your river of delights. For with you is the fountain of life: in your light we see light" (Ps 36:7–8). One of the sons [descendants] of Korah adds his voice: There is a river whose streams make glad the city of God, the holy place where the Most High dwells."[39] This finds its ultimate fulfillment in John's vision of the Holy City: "Then the angel showed me the river of the water of life, as clear as crystal, flowing from the throne of God and of the Lamb down the middle of the great street of the city. On each side of the river stood the tree of life, bearing twelve crops of fruit, yielding its fruit every month. And the leaves of the tree are for the healing of the nations" (Rev 22:1–3).[40]

The Apocalypse concludes with the returning and risen Lord extending an invitation: "Come! Let the one who is thirsty come; and let the one who wishes take the free gift of the water of life" (Rev 22:17). Early in Jesus' ministry, the woman at Jacob's well in Sychar came and asked him: "Sir, give me this water so that I won't get thirsty and have to keep coming here to draw water" (John 4:15). He granted her request. In John 8, the evangelist gives an extended account of Jesus' visit to Jerusalem for the autumn Festival of Tabernacles. He draws attention to a dramatic moment: "On the last and greatest day of the festival, Jesus stood and said in a loud voice, 'Let anyone who is thirsty come to me and drink. Whoever believes in me as Scripture has said, rivers of living water will flow from within them'" (John 7:37–38).[41] Don't worry, there's an inexhaustible supply of the water of life—free for the asking.

39. Ps 46:4. A similar picture emerges in Zech 14:8. Cf. Isa 12:3; Jer 17:13; Joel 3:18.

40. An allusion to Ezek 47:12.

41. For the background of this ritual, see Edersheim, *Temple*, 280–82.

10

Ezekiel and the New Testament

Ezekiel builds a prophetic bridge between the Testaments and makes the passage far smoother than it would have been without him.

—Hassell Bullock

INTRODUCTION

A casual reader might conclude that Ezekiel had little impact on the NT. But as pointed out numerous times in previous chapters, there are in fact some very significant influences on NT theology. This final chapter seeks to expand on these and pay tribute to the genius of Ezekiel.

As a starting point, here are the top five OT books directly quoted in the NT with the frequency in parentheses:

- Psalms (68)
- Isaiah (55)
- Deuteronomy (44)

- Genesis (35)
- Exodus (31)

So, how many direct quotes are there from Ezekiel? The United Bible Society's Greek New Testament lists only two direct quotes, Ezek 20:34, 41 in 2 Cor 6:17 and Ezek 37:27 in 2 Cor 6:16.[1] This may seem rather unpromising for further investigation, but the paucity of direct quotes is misleading since the book of Revelation has more allusions to Ezekiel than to any other book.[2] "Even this observation, however, doesn't do justice to the impact of Ezekiel on NT thought.[3] More specifically, one can show remarkable parallels and allusions between the teaching of Jesus and that of Ezekiel. . . . Indeed, among the prophets Ezekiel is as NT-oriented as any and more so than most."[4] This line of investigation offers more promise in connecting the dots between two individuals whose teaching, at first glance, may seem unrelated.

Bullock suggests two major concepts around which we may construct parallels between Ezekiel and Jesus, namely, the offices of prophet and priest.[5] Following up on his suggestion brings to light some striking correspondences.

EZEKIEL AND JESUS: PROPHETS OF THE LORD

Prophetic Call

Crucial to the office of prophet is the moment when Yahweh calls his servant into ministry. Each prophet is admitted to the divine council; they don't prophesy on the basis of their own imaginings

1. Aland et al., *Greek New Testament*, 899.

2. "The prophet is never acknowledged as the source of John's ideas, but there are dozens of direct contacts, and many more allusions, to Ezekiel" (Block, *Ezekiel*, 1:45).

3. For a brief summary, see Phinney, "Ezekiel," 620.

4. Bullock, "Ezekiel," 22.

5. Bullock, "Ezekiel," 22.

or dreams, like the false prophets, but rather Yahweh's word: "I will put my words in his mouth. He will tell them everything I command him" (Deut 18:18). And so, our two contemporary prophets, Jeremiah and Ezekiel, were summoned and charged with this solemn task: "You must go to everyone I send you to and say whatever I command you" (Jer 1:7). "You must speak my words to them, whether they listen or fail to listen" (Ezek 2:7–8).

Jesus' baptism in the Jordan River was his prophetic call to public ministry and exhibits features similar to Ezekiel's call. According to Matthew's Gospel, when Jesus came up out of the water, heaven was opened and the Spirit of God descended upon him like a dove. A voice from heaven conveyed divine approval: "You are my Son, whom I love: with you I am well pleased" (Luke 3:22).

Ezekiel experienced his call when he "was among the exiles by the Kebar River" (Ezek 1:1). In a vision, he was transported to the heavenly throne room. The one who sat on the throne and whose appearance was like "the glory of the LORD" directly addressed him: "Son of man, stand on your feet and I will speak to you" (Ezek 2:1). As he did so, "the Spirit came into me and raised me to my feet" (Ezek 2:2). "In no other OT prophetic call do we have the associations with the Spirit as we do in Ezekiel's experience. Further, we have no other instance in the OT where the heavens are opened to permit divine revelation."[6] Luke adds that Jesus was about thirty years old when he began his ministry" (3:23)—the same age as Ezekiel when he was called to be a prophet (Ezek 1:1). But the similarity of prophetic calls is just the tip of the iceberg—many more associations emerge from a close reading of the text.

Prophetic Speech

Both Ezekiel and Jesus employ allegories or parables in their messages. What makes this so striking is that in the OT prophetic

6. Bullock, "Ezekiel," 25.

books, this mode of communication appears almost exclusively in Ezekiel.[7]

In the Synoptic Gospels, Jesus preaches in parables. According to Mark, "He did not say anything to them without using a parable. But when he was alone with his disciples, he explained everything" (Mark 4:34). This practice was a source of puzzlement for his disciples: "Why do you speak to the people in parables" (Matt 13:10). Ezekiel likewise generated bewilderment among his listeners: "Sovereign Lord, they are saying of me, 'Isn't he just telling parables?'" (Ezek 20:49).

Ezekiel's allegory likening Jerusalem to a useless vine echoes in Jesus' allegory likening himself to a true vine and his disciples to its branches. To be sure, the audience and application differ, but the imagery employed makes a similar point. Ezekiel sums up his allegory of the useless vine with this warning, "And after it is thrown on the fire as fuel and the fire burns both ends and chars the middle, is it then useful for anything?" (Ezek 15:4). Jesus emphatically makes the same point for disciples who fall away: "apart from me you can do nothing . . . such branches are picked up, thrown into the fire and burned" (John 15:5–6).

Jesus' parable of the mustard seed similarly echoes Ezekiel's allegory of a cedar tree.[8] The common elements are as follows:

Mark	Ezekiel
"a mustard seed, which is the smallest of all seeds on earth" (4:31).	"a shoot from the very top of a cedar, . . . a tender sprig from its topmost shoots" (17:22).
"the birds can nest in its shade" (4:32).	"birds of every kind will nest in it" (17:23).

7. By my count there are ten allegories. See Ezek 15:1–8; 16:1–63; 17:1–24; 19:1–9, 10–14; 23:1–49; 24:1–14; 27:1–36; 31:1–18; 37:1–14. The distinction between an allegory and a parable is fluid and scholars are not agreed upon the definition of the respective genres. Nonetheless, between thirty and forty sayings of Jesus in the Synoptic Gospels may be designated as parables. See further Wright, "Parables" 559–62.

8. Mark 4:30–32; Ezek 17:22–24.

"it grows and becomes the largest of all garden plants" (4:32).	"it will . . . become a splendid cedar. . . . I the Lord bring down the tall tree and make the low tree grow tall" (17:24).

Another shared feature concerns the recognition formula "you shall know." This phrase occurs more than sixty times in the book of Ezekiel. "No other OT prophet put so much emphasis on a knowledge of the Lord as the normative relationship between man and God."[9] In John's Gospel this is also a major theme.[10] More than twenty times Jesus affirms that individuals or groups of people either know him or they don't.[11] Jesus' high priestly prayer for his disciples in chapter 17 underscores the point: "Now this is eternal life: *that they know you*, the only true God, and Jesus Christ whom you have sent" (John 17:3). Jesus' discourse in John 10:1–18 in which he identifies himself as "the good shepherd [who] lays down his life for the sheep" (John 10:11) recalls Ezekiel's earlier depiction of Yahweh as the shepherd of Israel.[12] What especially resonates from Ezekiel's parable is this climactic word of Yahweh: "Then *they will know* that I, the Lord their God, am with them and they, the Israelites, are my people, declares the Sovereign Lord" (Ezek 34:30). "Jesus used the same method and recognition formula in John's Gospel as did Ezekiel to establish the recognition of his relationship to the Father. The goal of his life and work, as with the prophet Ezekiel, was to bring men to the knowledge of God."[13]

9. Bullock, "Ezekiel," 27.

10. The circumstances surrounding John's Gospel helps us understand why this theme is so prominent in it. One of John's major purposes in writing his gospel was to counteract gnostic false teaching that touted itself as the exclusive possessor of true knowledge (*gnosis*). John adopts their terminology but infuses it with apostolic teaching.

11. See John 6:69; 7:17, 28–29; 8:14, 19, 37, 55; 19:4, 14, 15, 35; 13:17; 14:4–5, 7, 17, 20, 31; 16:30; 17:3, 7, 23.

12. Yahweh calls Israel "my flock" (Ezek 34:7, 10–11, 17, 22).

13. Bullock, "Ezekiel," 28.

Ezekiel's Unique Title

The attentive reader of Ezekiel's book also notices that Yahweh never addresses the prophet by his proper name, but rather as "son of man." This is an almost unique feature about Ezekiel among the OT prophets and stands quite in contrast to Ezekiel's contemporary Jeremiah.[14] Only Daniel, and that in one instance, is similarly addressed with the same meaning.[15] So, what does the expression mean? The Hebrew *ben adam* denotes a human being.[16] The expression connotes the frailty and mortality of mere mortals in contrast to the divine majesty of Yahweh—the everlasting, omnipotent God who sovereignly summons his human spokespersons and speaks his authoritative word to them.

In the Synoptic Gospels Jesus regularly refers to himself as Son of Man rather than Son of God or Messiah. Is it just a coincidence that Jesus shares this appellation with Ezekiel? I think a close reading reveals an intentional connection.

Ezekiel as a Suffering Servant

Ezekiel functions as a watchman for his people Israel. This task necessarily identifies him with those for whom he is responsible. He is not an outsider; he is one of them. The bond between prophet and people assumes prominence during his first symbolic act. In the sight of his fellow Jews, he symbolically bears the sin of Israel and Judah by lying first on his left side for 390 days (Israel) and then on his right side forty days (Judah), a day for each year of their national sin. During this time, he portends the horrific siege of Jerusalem, eating and drinking just enough to stay alive. At the end of this grueling regimen, the people in the camp are appalled

14. See, e.g., Jer 1:11 and 24:1 where he is directly addressed by his name. All the other references to his name are in third person but never is the title "son of man" used in third-person references.

15. Dan 8:14.

16. *DCH*, 2:206.

at his appearance, a mere shell of a man. No other prophet goes to such lengths to share in the sufferings of his people.

Whereas Isaiah *foresees* the vicarious suffering of the Servant of the Lord, Ezekiel *experiences* vicarious suffering because of the sins of Yahweh's people. Even the manner in which he "bears" the sin of Israel and Judah is freighted with typological significance, that is, he silently submits to the divinely mandated suffering. Isaiah prophesied about the silent, suffering Servant of the Lord: "He was oppressed and afflicted, yet he did not open his mouth; he was led like a lamb to the slaughter, and as a sheep before its shearers is silent, so he did not open his mouth" (Isa 53:7). But Ezekiel, a servant of the Lord, personally suffered in silent obedience: "you will be silent and unable to rebuke them, for they are a rebellious people" (3:26). As Bullock points out, "Ezekiel parts company with the other OT prophets, for they more or less stood outside of Israel and preached to her but did not give the impression of being one with her."[17]

Ezekiel the Judge of Israel

In the NT one of the primary eschatological functions of Jesus as the Son of Man is to render final judgment (Matt 25:31–46; Mark 8:38//Matt 16:27; Luke 9:26). What is interesting is that Yahweh commands only Ezekiel among the OT prophets to pass judgment upon Israel. "Will you judge them? Will you judge them, son of man?" (Ezek 20:4a). The rhetorical question expects a positive reply because Yahweh immediately orders the prophet "to confront them with the detestable practices of their ancestors" (Ezek 20:4b). The summons to judge (in Yahweh's name) is followed by a historical litany of Israel's apostasy. In two other passages Yahweh orders the prophet, addressed as "son of man," to pass judgment upon a rebellious and unfaithful people: "Will you judge her [Jerusalem]" (20:4) and "Will you judge Oholah [Israel] and Oholibah [Judah]" (23:36). One hears an echo of these passages in John's Gospel in

17. Bullock, "Ezekiel," 29.

which Jesus says to the hostile Jewish leaders: "For as the Father has life in himself, so he has granted the Son also to have life in himself. And he has given him authority to judge because he is the Son of Man" (John 5:27).[18]

EZEKIEL AND JESUS AS PRIESTS

As earlier noted, Ezekiel combines the offices of priest and prophet in his ministry.[19] So does Jesus. Although the Gospels don't draw out explicit priestly functions in their portraits of Jesus, the book of Hebrews does so by presenting Jesus as the great high priest after the order of Melchizedek. Ezekiel doesn't prefigure this aspect of Jesus' ministry, but he does share with Jesus priestly concerns.

Vicarious Suffering

The first priestly action we read in Ezekiel's book involves his elaborate and extended symbolic action previewing Yahweh's judgment on the rebellious city of Jerusalem. In the mime, Ezekiel doesn't offer a sacrifice for sin, but he does bear the sin of Israel and Judah by lying first on his left side and then his right. While not actually atoning for Israel and Judah's sin, this dramatic action prefigures Jesus' action as "the Lamb of God who takes away the sin of the world" (John 1:29; cf. 1 John 2:2). Hebrews affirms that "Christ was sacrificed once to take away the sins of many, and he will appear a second time, *not to bear sin*, but to bring salvation to those who are waiting for him" (Heb 9:28). Whereas Isaiah with his incomparable poetry prophesies that the Suffering Servant "bore our suffering" (Isa 53:4; cf. v. 5) and "bore the sin of many" (53:12;

18. The Greek expression (*huios anthropou*) corresponds precisely to the Hebrew expression for Ezekiel (*ben adam*).

19. Ezekiel isn't unique in being both a priest and prophet, since Jeremiah also shared that status. Zechariah the son of Berechiah and grandson of Iddo, a post-exilic prophet and contemporary of Zerubbabel, was also from a priestly family (Zech 1:1).

cf. v. 11), only Ezekiel among the prophets acts out the bearing of his people's sin *in his own body*.

Zeal for a Purified Temple

Ezekiel's visionary visit to the Jerusalem temple was a downer. Five times Yahweh asked him, "Son of man, do you see what they are doing—the utterly detestable things the Israelites are doing here?" (8:6, 9, 12, 15, 17). Idolatry, injustice, and iniquity would drive Yahweh from his temple and provoke his wrath, which when poured out, would meet with utter indifference to cries for help: "Although they shout in my ears, I will not listen to them" (8:18). The prospect of Yahweh's impending judgment—six destroying angels armed with weapons and commissioned to kill without mercy or compassion "old men, the young men and women, the mothers and their children"—so unnerved the prophet he cried out with a loud voice: "Alas, Sovereign Lord! Are you going to destroy the entire remnant of Israel in this outpouring of your wrath on Jerusalem?" (9:8; 11:1).

Ezekiel's anguished question receives an answer: a remnant will survive, loyal followers of Yahweh bearing a mark on their foreheads and grieving and lamenting "over all the detestable things that are done in [Jerusalem]" (Ezek 9:6). Not only will they survive, they will return: "I will gather you from the nations and bring you back . . . to the land of Israel again" (Ezek 11:17). Ezekiel's zeal for Yahweh's house would be realized beyond his wildest dreams—a new, magnificent, purified temple would arise and Yahweh would forever dwell in it with his redeemed people.

Jesus' actual visit to Herod's Temple was also a downer. When he witnessed buying and selling of sacrificial animals and money changing in the temple courts, he made a whip of cords and drove out the sheep and cattle and overturned the tables of the money changers. To the dove merchants he yelled, "Get these out of here! Stop making my Father's house into a market!" (John 2:16). The evangelist adds this comment: "His disciples remembered that it is written: 'Zeal for your house will consume me'" (John 1:17).[20]

In addition to the crass commercialization of the temple, the religious leaders compounded their sin by rejecting Jesus' teaching. Filled with animosity, they challenged him to authenticate both his parentage and his preaching. As to the former they hurled the slander of illegitimacy; as to the latter they accused him of blasphemy. His miracles were written off because he was in league with Beelzebub (Satan).[21]

So, what would happen to the "massive stones" and "magnificent buildings" of Herod's Temple so admired by Jesus' disciples? "Truly I tell you, not one stone here will be left on another; every one will be thrown down" (Matt 24:2). And what about the people who lived in Jerusalem? The temple and city would be destroyed and its population decimated.[22] In 586 BC, a remnant survived the siege.[23] In AD 70, believers in Messiah Jesus were spared the siege. "When you see Jerusalem being surrounded by armies, . . . flee to the mountains, let those in the city get out" (Luke 21:20–21). According to the early church historian Eusebius, the believers fled to Pella, across the Jordan, where they established a number of churches and flourished.[24]

But there is more. Although the Romans threw down the stones of Herod's Temple in AD 70, the risen Lord was already building a new and more glorious temple. At his first visit to the temple, the religious leaders challenged him to authenticate his actions. Jesus responded: "Destroy this temple, and I will raise it up in three days" (John 2:19). John explains that Jesus was really referring to his body (2:21). During his last visit to Jerusalem, Jesus put

20. A quotation of Ps 69:9.

21. See John 8:12–59.

22. See Matt 22:1–7 and esp. Luke 21:20–24.

23. Two of those survivors were Jeremiah and his faithful scribe Baruch (Jer 43:6).

24. "The whole body, however, of the church at Jerusalem, having been commanded by a divine revelation, given to men of approved piety there before the war, removed from the city, and dwelt at a certain town beyond the Jordan, called Pella" (Eusebius, *Hist. eccl.* 3.5.3.[trans. C. F. Cruse]).

this question to the chief priests and Pharisees: "Have you never read in the Scriptures: 'The stone the builders rejected has become the cornerstone; the Lord has done this, and it is marvelous in our eyes'?" (Matt 21:42). These two sayings are foundational for the doctrine of the church as the body of Christ.

The apostles Paul and Peter develop this further. Jesus' new temple isn't a limestone structure adorned with marble and gilded with gold; it's his mystical body, the church. Individual members are "built on the foundation of the prophets and apostles, with Jesus Christ himself as the chief cornerstone. In him the whole building is joined together and rises to become *a holy temple* in the Lord. And in him you too [the gentiles] are being built together to become a dwelling in which God lives by the Spirit" (Eph 2:20–22). Peter adds this vivid touch when he likens believers to "living stones . . . being built into a spiritual house" (1 Pet 2:5). And this spiritual building is invincible: "I will build my church, and the gates of Hades will not overcome it" (Matt 16:18; cf. Eph 6:10–18).

Even though external enemies can't destroy Christ's church, internal corruption can cause great harm. Just as Ezekiel was appalled by the moral and spiritual depravity of the Jerusalemites of his day, so too was Paul appalled by the immaturity and worldliness of many Corinthian believers who were swept up in jealousy, quarreling, and bitter rivalry. Paul's pointed question to the congregation highlights their spiritual failure: "Don't you know that you yourselves are God's temple and that God's Spirit dwells in your midst? If anyone destroys God's temple, God will destroy that person; for God's temple is sacred, and *you together are that temple*" (1 Cor 3:16–17).[25]

But the situation at Corinth was even more serious. Sexual immorality was seeping into the congregation like sewer gas, threatening the spiritual health of the Corinthian house churches. "It is actually reported that there is sexual immorality among you and of a kind that even pagans do not tolerate: A man is sleeping with his father's wife" (1 Cor 5:1). Paul directs another pointed

25. It should be noted that the pronouns are plural, referring to the corporate nature of the spiritual temple, the church.

question at the believers: "Do you not know that *your bodies are the temples of the Holy Spirit*, who is in you, whom you have received from God? You are not your own; you were bought with a price. Therefore honor God with your bodies" (1 Cor 6:19–20).[26]

Peter chimes in with a reminder to his readers, who, like Ezekiel's audience, were exiles (1 Pet 1:1).[27] "For it is time for judgment to *begin with God's household*; and if it begins with us, what will the outcome be for those who do not obey the gospel of God?" (1 Pet 4:17). The echo from Ezek 9:6: "*Begin at my sanctuary*" is unmistakable.

Whereas Ezekiel foresaw a new and larger temple, Jesus foresaw a newer and even larger temple—one that transcends earthly limitations, takes on cosmic proportions, and transposes the material into the spiritual. Listen to Paul extol the cosmic dimensions of Christ's church: "And God placed all things under his feet and appointed him to be head over the church, which is his body, the fullness of him who fills everything in every way" (Eph 1:22–23). "His intent was that now, through the church, the manifold wisdom of God should be made known to the rulers and authorities in the heavenly realms, according to his eternal purpose that he accomplished in Christ Jesus our Lord" (Eph 3:10–11). John's climactic vision in the Apocalypse adds the final touches to redemptive history and in so doing comforts all who yearn for the new Jerusalem: "God's dwelling place is now among the people and they will dwell with him" (Rev 21:3). But note carefully—there is no splendid building in the Holy City. And why not? Because "*the Lord God Almighty and the Lamb are its temple*" (Rev 21:22).

To authenticate the veracity of his vision, the one "seated on the throne," instructed John, "Write this down, for these words are trustworthy and true" (Rev 21:5). In this we hear an echo from Ezekiel's climactic vision: "Write these down before them so that

26. The pronouns in this passage are singular, referring to individual members.

27. They weren't in Babylon but rather "scattered throughout the provinces of Pontus, Galatia, Cappadocia, Asia, and Bithynia" (1 Pet 1:1), lying within the territory of modern Turkey.

they may be faithful to its design and follow all its regulations" (Ezek 43:11). Like Ezekiel and John, Isaiah's grand vision of an eternal king reigning over an eternal kingdom concludes with a trustworthy promise: "The zeal of the LORD Almighty will accomplish this" (Isa 9:7).

EZEKIEL AND THE DOCTRINE OF BODILY RESURRECTION

Ezekiel's vision of the dry bones left a lasting legacy in both Judaism and Christianity. The Pharisees derived from it the doctrine of bodily resurrection for individual Jews.[28] It was but a small step from the expectation of a national restoration—pictured as the reassembly of scattered bones into skeletons and the resuscitation of corpses to living human beings—to the full-blown doctrine of individual bodily resurrection at the day of the LORD.

Jesus emphatically rejected the Sadducean denial of bodily resurrection: "You are in error" (Matt 22:29; see also vv. 30–32). The apostles followed the Master and unequivocally affirmed this teaching. The apostle Paul (and pharisee)[29] could even say, "For what I received I passed on to you *as of first importance:* that Christ died for our sins according to the Scriptures, that he was buried, that *he was raised on the third day* according to the Scriptures, and that he appeared to Cephas, and then to the Twelve" (1 Cor 15:3). For Paul the truthfulness of the gospel was at stake. "If Christ has not been raised, your faith is futile; you are still in your sins" (1 Cor 15:14). The latest NT documents, John's Gospel and the

28. Explicit mention of bodily resurrection first appears in Dan 12:2, generally dated to shortly after 165 BC. Many also see earlier intimations in Job 19:25–27; Pss 16:9–11; 73:24–26; and Isa 25:7–8. And in the Apocrypha, 2 Macc 7:9, 11, usually dated between 104 and 63 BC, unambiguously affirms this teaching (Helyer, *Jewish Literature*, 163). And 4 Macc 18:17 (probably mid-first century AD and contemporary with Paul) also refers to bodily resurrection, based on Ezekiel's vision of the dry bones.

29. See Acts 23:6; Phil 3:5.

Apocalypse, clearly teach the doctrine of bodily resurrection for both the righteous and the wicked.[30]

Rabbinic Judaism, the successor of Pharisaism, affirmed bodily resurrection for the righteous at judgment day. In the Middle Ages, Maimonides (AD 1138–1204) included it in his thirteen affirmations, binding on every Jew. In short, both orthodox Judaism and orthodox Christianity share a commitment to the doctrine of bodily resurrection, and Ezekiel's vision of the dry bones played a role in validating this belief.[31]

THE THRONE ROOM

An obvious allusion to the book of Ezekiel occurs in John's throne-room vision.[32] Like Ezekiel, who saw flashing lightning, brilliant light, glowing metal, and fire surrounding Yahweh's throne-chariot, John stood before a celestial throne surrounded with flashes of lightning and seven blazing lamps. Even more striking is the common reference to a radiant rainbow around the one who sits on the throne and four living creatures at the center of the throne room.

EATING A SCROLL

In the interlude between the sixth and seventh trumpets, the Patmos seer has two visionary experiences, both of which resonate with Ezekelian precursors. In the first, an angel commands him to eat a little scroll, tasting "sweet as honey" in his mouth, but turning his "stomach sour" (Rev 10:9–10). This recalls Yahweh's commanding Ezekiel to eat a scroll that "tasted as sweet as honey" (Ezek 2:3). Though not immediately causing a sour stomach, Ezekiel's inaugural vision ends with the prophet "in bitterness" (3:14).

30. John 5:25–29; 11:23–25; Rev 20:4–5, 12–13.

31. Reform Judaism, the largest "denomination" in American Jewry provides no clear-cut or official guidance on this point. Some believe in the survival of the soul after death whereas others deny any continuing conscious life whatsoever.

32. Rev 4:1–11; Ezek 1:4–28.

There is a further point of both comparison and contrast. After eating the scroll, both Ezekiel and John were commissioned to prophesy. Ezekiel's audience, however, was limited "to the people of Israel" (Ezek 3:5) whereas John was charged to prophesy "about many peoples, nations, languages and kings" (Rev 10:11). The ethnocentric character of Ezekiel's ministry stands in contrast to the universality of John's prophecy.

GOG AND MAGOG

An unmistakable Ezekelian echo in the Apocalypse resonates in the Gog and Magog prophecy.[33] John places the invasion of "the camp of God's people, the city he loves" (Rev 20:9) "when the thousand years are over" (Rev 20:7). This answers to Yahweh's word to Ezekiel concerning Gog: "*After many days* you will be called to arms. *In future years* you will invade a land that has recovered from war, whose people were gathered from many nations to the mountains of Israel, which had long been desolate. They had been brought out from the nations, and "now all of them live in safety" (Ezek 38:8; cf. v. 11, "a peaceful and unsuspecting people").

Both prophets graphically describe the outcome of this demonically inspired invasion. Ezekiel goes into much more detail: plague, bloodshed, rain, hailstones, and burning sulfur pour down on Gog's hordes. Yahweh even incinerates Gog's allies on the coastlands. The upshot is massive loss of life requiring seven months to bury the corpses, or at least what's left after the birds and wild animals gorge themselves on the carrion (38:22—39:20). The Apocalypse offers an abbreviated version of the battle over the Holy City: "fire came from heaven and devoured them. And the devil, who deceived them, was thrown into the lake of burning sulfur" (Rev 20:9). Short, but not sweet.

The aftermath of Gog's invasion in Ezekiel focuses upon Israel's recognition of Yahweh, the nations' realization of Yahweh's purpose in punishing Israel, and Israel's restoration to her ancestral

33. Rev 20:7–10.

land, which lasts forever. The Apocalypse features an equivalent to Ezekiel: Everyone finally acknowledges God's holiness, justice, and truth when they stand before him at the final judgment. Following this, John sees the new heaven and new earth, with its centerpiece, "the Holy City, the new Jerusalem" (21:2). There God will dwell with his people forever.

MEASURING THE TEMPLE

I draw attention to one more common feature, namely, recording or measuring a visionary temple. Ezekiel dutifully follows his angelic guide, "whose appearance was like bronze" and who had "a linen cord and a measuring rod in his hand" (40:3). The tour begins with the outer wall and its gates and moves inward to the temple itself. At each stop, the prophet writes down the various measurements. The tour concludes with a measurement of the entire complex, an area encompassing five hundred cubits designed "to separate the holy from the common" (42:20).[34]

In the interlude between the sixth and seventh trumpets, John was told: "Go and measure the temple of God and the altar, with its worshipers" (Rev 11:1). No measurements, however, are recorded. The temporal placement of this temple is problematic; the text says the temple will be trampled down by the gentiles for forty-two months.[35] For that reason it can't be the same temple Ezekiel saw. Furthermore, in John's vision, there is no temple in the Holy City. Instead, with a golden rod, John measures "the city,

34. According to the Mishnah, surrounding the central courtyard of the Second Temple (called the Azarah) was a large square courtyard measuring five hundred cubits (*Mid.* 2.1). Leen Ritmyer believes one can still see some of the wall from this structure (Ritmeyer and Ritmeyer, *Secrets*, 65–97). Converted to feet this area measures ca. 750 sq. ft.

35. The literature on this point in dispensational circles is voluminous. The temple John was to measure in Rev 11 may be the same one referred to in passing by the Apostle in 2 Thess 2:4 in which the man of lawlessness (the Antichrist) demands to be worshiped as God. This is probably the temple Jesus referred to in Matt 24:15: "So when you see standing in the holy place 'the abomination that causes desolation,' spoken of through the prophet Daniel."

its gates and its walls," a massive cube of about 1,400 miles (Rev 21:15–16), thus replicating the three-dimensional symmetry of the Holy of Holies in the tabernacle and temple.

NEW COVENANT AND INDIVIDUAL RESPONSIBILITY

In addition to the above-mentioned echoes, two theological truths lying at the heart of NT theology first appear in Ezekiel. In fact, our dynamic duo, Ezekiel and Jeremiah, perform a prophetic duet announcing them: a new covenant and individual responsibility for one's spiritual standing before God. Let's see how this plays out.

New Covenant

Ezekiel, like all the OT prophets, harps on Israel's repeated violations of the Sinai covenant stipulations. After putting Israel on notice for non-compliance and exercising extraordinary forbearance, Yahweh reluctantly enforces the ultimate sanction for disloyalty, expulsion from the land of promise.[36]

The exile was Israel's long overdue punishment for failure to observe that most basic stipulation of the Sinai covenant: "You shall have no other gods before me. You shall not make for yourself an image in the form of anything in heaven above or on the earth beneath or in the water below" (Exod 20:3–4).

But after sentencing Israel to hard labor in exile for seventy years, Yahweh has compassion and initiates something extraordinary—he will regather and return them to their ancient homeland. There on "the mountains of Israel" (Ezek 36:1) he sanctifies and regenerates his people: "I will cleanse you from all your impurities and from all your idols. I will give you a new heart and put a new spirit in you; I will remove from you your heart of stone and give

36. The rupture between Yahweh and his people is sometimes pictured as a divorce. Both Hosea and Jeremiah employ this imagery. See Hos 2:2–13; Jer 3:1.

you a heart of flesh. And I will put my Spirit in you and move you to follow my decrees and be careful to keep my laws" (36:25–26).

This amazing makeover is part of a new arrangement, a new covenant, between Yahweh and Israel: "I will establish an everlasting covenant with you" (16:60), "a covenant of peace" (34:25). Jeremiah calls it a new covenant, "not like the covenant I made with their ancestors . . . because they broke my covenant. . . . I will put my law in their minds and write it on their hearts" (Jer 31:32–33). In this new covenant, Yahweh addresses the underlying problem, hardness of heart, and, in a manner of speaking, performs a heart transplant and a Spirit implant: "I will remove from you your heart of stone and give you a heart of flesh. And I will put my Spirit in you" (36:26–27). The result is obedience and restoration in a land that becomes "like the garden of Eden" (36:35).

The exilic promise of a new covenant, announced by Jeremiah and Ezekiel, is fulfilled in the NT and constitutes the relationship between Christ and his church, the "chosen people, [a] royal priesthood, a holy nation, God's special possession, . . . the people of God" (1 Pet 2:9–10). In fact, the New *Testament* is better designated the New *Covenant.*

The new covenant theme permeates the NT. On the night of the Last Supper Jesus told his disciples, "This cup is the new covenant in my blood, which is poured out for you" (Luke 22:20). The next day he shed his blood on the cross and "entered the most Holy Place once for all by his own blood, thus obtaining eternal redemption" (Heb 8:12). Hebrews doubles down on the same point as Jeremiah and Ezekiel, namely, the superiority of the new covenant because it "is established on better promises" (Heb 8:6). The apostle Paul describes himself and his missionary team "as ministers of a new covenant—not of the letter but of the Spirit, for the letter kills, but the Spirit gives life" (2 Cor 3:6). In his polemical letter to the Galatians, Paul argues at length the inferiority of the old Sinai covenant in that it enslaves rather than liberates.[37]

37. Gal 4:21—5:6.

Individual Responsibility

A further teaching, first introduced in the OT by Ezekiel and Jeremiah, must be mentioned because it too, like the new covenant, lies at the heart of NT thought. Both prophets confront an attitude among their contemporaries that sounds familiar today. The Jerusalem remnant and the exiles in Babylon sought to shift the blame for their misfortunes. Distorting the truth in the notion of corporate solidarity, both communities rationalized by hiding behind a popular proverb: "The parents eat sour grapes, and the children's teeth are set on edge" (Ezek 18:2). The point of the proverb was to shift the blame for wrongdoing and its consequences to ancestors and parents.

Both prophets push back and insist that "the one who sins is the one who will die" (Ezek 18:3; cf. Jer 31:29). The ramifications of individual responsibility are significant.

1. No person may blame others for his or her sin; each is personally responsible. In short, "each individual is master of his or her own destiny."[38]
2. No person may appeal to a doctrine of eternal security that is fixed and unchangeable based on choices and decisions made in the past. Ezekiel's appeal to repent and live assumes "a real personal freedom to determine at any time not only one's own conduct but also the destiny that God decrees for a person."[39]
3. No person may accuse God of injustice and unfairness in judgment. The psalmist celebrates God's fairness: "he will judge the people with equity" (Ps 96:10; cf. Ps 98:9). To Abram's anguished question, "Will not the judge of all the earth do right?" there is an affirmative answer: He will. God does not cause a person to sin, "for all have sinned and fall

38. Block, *Ezekiel*, 1:589.

39. Block, *Ezekiel*, 1:590. He doesn't commit to either a Calvinist or Arminian interpretation of the nature of God's decree. He is content to say, "this statement is silent on Yahweh's effectual keeping power of the believer."

short of the glory of God" (Rom 3:23). Rather, he "wants all people to be saved and to come to a knowledge of the truth" (1 Tim 2:3). "Furthermore, "he is patient . . . , not wanting anyone to perish, but everyone to come to repentance" (2 Pet 3:9). Nor does God deny sufficient grace to everyone to respond to his saving grace "for the grace of God has appeared *that offers salvation to all people*" (Titus 2:11).[40]

4. The NT everywhere assumes individual responsibility. Here are three (among many) instances: "So then, each of us will give an account of ourselves to God" (Rom 14:12). "Everything is uncovered and laid bare before the eyes of him to whom we must give account" (Heb 4:13). The famous vision of the great white throne underscores this truth: "each person was judged according to what they had done" (Rev 20:13).
5. Individual accountability extends beyond theology. In politics, representative democracy stands or falls on the principle of personal accountability. Without accountability, government is vulnerable to authoritarianism. And when this happens, personal and partisan self-interest redefine the common good. This is a real and present danger in the current political climate in which the number of democracies worldwide is diminishing and political pundits in the United States are sounding an alarm about the fragility of our own representative democracy.

TRIBUTE TO WHOM TRIBUTE IS DUE

Ezekiel doesn't generally receive the recognition he deserves for his contribution to prophetic literature and to the NT. In some respects, he sits in the shadow of his more illustrious predecessor Isaiah, whose poetry and prose are peerless. Even Jeremiah,

40. This ability is entirely owing to God's prevenient grace (grace that goes before and prepares the heart to receive the good news). *Prevenient* grace, however, is not *irresistible* grace. Sadly, many reject this grace and persist in their rebellion and sin.

Ezekiel's contemporary comrade in arms, receives more accolades than Ezekiel.

But I hope I've convinced readers that the book of Ezekiel has many merits for those willing to read and ponder the words Yahweh gave him. Like the book of Jeremiah, the book of Ezekiel is a book of *hope*, something in short supply during these hard times of pandemic and political partisanship.[41] I hope the reader of my short book will not opt for a short cut and bypass reading the words of the inspired prophet himself.

I conclude this book with a challenge from a scholar who has spent years reading, studying, teaching, and writing a two-volume commentary on the book of Ezekiel (1,544 pages!). "For all who are willing to engage this most mysterious of Israel's prophets, the rewards are inestimable."[42] I wholeheartedly agree.

41. See my concluding comments on Jeremiah in Helyer, *Jeremiah*, 125–26.

42. Block, *Ezekiel*, 1:46.

Bibliography on Ezekiel

Aland, Kurt, et al., eds. *The Greek New Testament*. 3rd ed. Münster: United Bible Societies, 1975.

Aleichum, Sholem. *Tevya's Daughters: Collected Stories of Sholem Aleichum*. Translated by Frances Butwin. No loc. Sholem Aleichum Family, 1999.

Alexander, Ralph H. *Ezekiel*. EBC 6. Grand Rapids: Zondervan, 1986.

———. "A Fresh Look at Ezekiel 38 and 39." *JETS* 17 (1974) 155–69.

Allen, Leslie C. *Ezekiel 1–19*. WBC 28. Dallas: Word, 1994.

——— *Ezekiel 20–48*. WBC 29. Dallas: Word, 1990.

Arnold, Patrick M. "Ramoth-Gilead." In *ABD* 5:620–21.

Barker, Glenn W., et al. *The New Testament Speaks*. New York: Harper & Row, 1969.

Bella, Timothy. "Pat Robertson Says Putin Was 'Compelled by God' to Invade Ukraine to Fulfill Armageddon Prophecy." *The Washington Post*, March 1, 2022. https://www.washingtonpost.com/world/2022/03/01/pat-robertson-putin-god-russia-ukraine/.

Blenkinsopp, Joseph. *Ezekiel*. Interpretation. Louisville: John Knox, 1990.

Block, Daniel. I. *The Book of Ezekiel Chapters 1–24*. NICOT. Grand Rapids: Eerdmans, 1997.

———. *The Book of Ezekiel Chapters 25–48*. NICOT. Grand Rapids: Eerdmans, 1997.

Boadt, Lawrence. "Ezekiel, the Book of." In *ABD* 2:711–16.

Bullock, C. H. "Ezekiel, Bridge between the Testaments." *JETS* 25 (1982) 22–31.

Däniken, Erich von. *Chariots of the Gods?* Berlin: Econ-Verlag, 1968.

Duguid, Iain M. *Ezekiel*. The NIV Application Commentary. Grand Rapids: Zondervan, 1999. Ebook.

Duty, Guy. *If Ye Continue*. Minneapolis: Bethany, 1966.

Duvall, J. Scott, and J. Daniel Hays. "Ezekiel." In *The Baker Illustrated Bible Background Commentary*, edited by J. Scott Duvall and J. Daniel Hays, 581. Grand Rapids: Baker, 2020.

Dyer, Charles H. "Ezekiel." In *An Exposition of the Scriptures by Dallas Faculty*, edited by Roy B. Zuck, 1224–1321. Colorado Springs: Scripture Press, 1983.

Edersheim, Alfred. *The Temple: Its Ministry and Services as They Were in the Time of Christ*. London: James Clarke, 1959.

Ellison, H. L. *Ezekiel: The Man and His Message*. Grand Rapids: Eerdmans, 1956.

Elwell, Walter A., ed. "Seraph, Seraphim." In *BEB* 2:1926–27.

Fee, Gordon D., and Douglas Stuart. *How to Read the Bible for All Its Worth*. 3rd ed. Grand Rapids: Zondervan, 2003.

Feinberg, Charles L. *Ezekiel*. EBC 6. Grand Rapids: Zondervan, 1986.

———. *The Prophecy of Ezekiel: The Glory of the Lord*. 1969. Reprint, Eugene, OR: Wipf & Stock, 2003.

Fischer, Austin. *Young, Restless, No Longer Reformed*. Eugene, OR: Cascade, 2014.

Gesenius, Wilhelm. *Hebrew-Chaldee Lexicon of the Old Testament Scriptures*. 1809. Reprint, Grand Rapids: Baker, 1979.

Glueck, Nelson. "Ramoth-Gilead." *BASOR* 92 (1943) 10–16.

Grenz, Stanley. *The Millennial Maze*. Downers Grove, IL: InterVarsity, 1992.

Hall, Bert H. "Jeremiah, Lamentations, Ezekiel and Daniel." In *The Wesleyan Bible Commentary*, edited by Charles Carter et al., 3:365–497. Grand Rapids: Eerdmans, 1969.

Helyer, Larry R. *Exploring Jewish Literature of the Second Temple Period*. Downers Grove, IL: InterVarsity, 2002.

———. *The Life and Witness of David*. Eugene, OR: Cascade, 2020.

———. *The Life and Witness of Jeremiah*. Eugene, OR: Cascade, 2019.

———. *Mountaintop Theology*. Eugene, OR: Cascade, 2016.

———. "Queries & Comments: Explains Order to Forge Chains in Ezekiel 7:23." *BAR* 10 (1984) 18.

———. *Yesterday, Today and Forever*. 2nd ed. Salem, WI: Sheffield, 2004.

Kelle, Brad E. *Ezekiel: A Commentary in the Wesleyan Tradition*. Kansas City, MO: Beacon Hill, 2013.

Ladd, George Eldon. *A Theology of the New Testament*. Rev. ed. Edited by Donald A. Hagner. Grand Rapids: Eerdmans, 1993.

Letham, Robert W. A. "Reformed Theology." In *New Dictionary of Theology*, 569–72. Downers Grove, IL: InterVarsity, 1988.

Lewis, C. S. *The Lion, the Witch, and the Wardrobe*. 1950. Reprint, New York: HarperCollins, 2000.

Life Application Study Bible. Grand Rapids: Zondervan/Carol Stream: Tyndale House, 2011.

Lindsey, Hal. *The Late Great Planet Earth*. Grand Rapids: Zondervan, 1970.

———. *There's a New World Coming*. Eugene, OR: Harvest House, 1984.

Longman, Tremper, III, and Daniel P. Reid. *God Is a Warrior*. Grand Rapids: Zondervan, 1995.

Luther, Martin. *Luther's Works*. Vol. 54, *Table Talk*. Edited by Helmut T. Lehmann. Philadelphia: Fortress, 1967.

Marshall, I. Howard. *Kept by the Power of God*. Minneapolis: Bethany Fellowship, 1969.

Motyer, J. Alec. *Isaiah: An Introduction and Commentary.* TOTC 20. Downers Grove, IL: InterVarsity, 1999.

Oden, Thomas C. *The Transforming Power of Grace.* Nashville: Abingdon, 1993.

Petersen, David L. "Ezekiel: Introduction." In *The HarperCollins Study Bible*, edited by Wayne A. Meeks et al., 1222–24. New York: HarperCollins, 1993.

Peterson, Eugene H. *The Pastor: A Memoir.* San Francisco: HarperOne, 2012.

Phinney, D. Nathan. "Ezekiel, Book of." In *The Eerdmans Dictionary of Early Judaism*, edited by John J. Collins and Danie C. Harlow, 619–20. Grand Rapids: Eerdmans, 2010.

Picirilli, Robert E. *Understanding Assurance & Salvation.* Nashville: Randall, 2006. Ebook.

Pope, William Burt. *Compendium of Christian Theology.* 3 vols. London: Wesleyan Conference Office, 1877–79.

Pritchard, James, B., ed. *The Ancient Near East in Pictures Relating to the Old Testament.* 2nd ed. Princeton: Princeton University Press, 1969.

Purkiser, W. T. *The Book of Psalms.* BBC. Kansas City: Beacon Hill, 1980.

Richards, Lawrence O. *The Bible Reader Companion.* Wheaton, IL: Victor, 1991. Ebook.

———. *The Teacher's Commentary.* Wheaton, IL: Scripture, 1987.

Ritmeyer, Leen, and Kathleen Ritmeyer. *Secrets of Jerusalem's Temple Mount.* Washington, DC: Biblical Archaeological Society, 1998.

Robertson, Pat. *The End of the Age.* Nashville: Nelson, 1995.

Rooker, Mark F. *Biblical Hebrew in Transition: The Language of the Book of Ezekiel.* JSOTSup 90. Sheffield: JSOT Press, 1990.

Rowdon, H. H. "Dispensationalism." In *New Dictionary of Theology*, edited by David Wright et al., 201. Downers Grove, IL: Inter-Varsity, 1988.

Ryken, Leland. *Reading the Bible as Literature.* Bellingham, WA: Lexham, 2016.

Ryrie, Charles. *Dispensationalism Today.* Chicago: Moody, 1965.

Shank, Robert. *Life in the Son.* Springfield, MO: Westcott, 1960.

Shiloh, Yigal. "Jerusalem: The Early Periods and the First Temple Period: Excavation Results." In *The New Encyclopedia of Archaeological Excavations in the Holy Land*, edited by Ephraim Stern et al., 2:701–12. Jerusalem: Israel Exploration Society & Carta, 1993.

Smith, Gary V. "Seraphim." In *ISBE* 4:410–11.

Stuart, Douglas. *Ezekiel.* The Preacher's Commentary 20. Nashville: Thomas Nelson, 1989.

Sweeney, Marvin A. "Ezekiel." In *The Jewish Study Bible*, edited by Adele Berlin and Marc Zvi Brettler, 1042–45. Oxford: Oxford University Press, 2004.

Taylor, John B. *Ezekiel: An Introduction and Commentary.* TOTC 22. Downers Grove, IL: InterVarsity, 1969.

Traina, Robert A. *Methodical Bible Study.* Wilmore, KY: Traina, 1980.

Walton, John H. "Ezekiel." In *IVP Bible Background Commentary: Old Testament*, n.p. Downers Grove, IL: InterVarsity, 2000. Ebook.

Wesley, John. *The Works of John Wesley.* Vol. 10, *The Methodist Societies, the Minutes of Conference.* Edited by Randy L. Maddox. Nashville: Abingdon, 2011.

Westcott, B. F. *The Gospel According to St. John.* London: John Murray, 1903.

The Westminster Shorter Catechism in Modern English. Edited by Kevin Bidwell. Welwyn Garden City, UK: Evangelical, 2019.

Wiersbe, Warren W. *Be Reverent: Bowing before Our Awesome God.* Colorado Springs: Cook, 2000.

———. *Ezekiel: Bowing before Our Awesome God.* Colorado Springs: Cook, 2014.

Wilson, Clifford. *Crash Go the Chariots.* New York: Lancer, 1972.

Wise, Michael, et al., eds. *The Dead Sea Scrolls: A New Translation.* San Francisco: HarperSanFrancisco, 1996.

Wright, Christopher J. H. *The Message of Ezekiel: A New Heart and a New Start.* Downers Grove, IL: InterVarsity, 2001.

Wright, Stephen I. "Parables." In *Dictionary for Theological Interpretation of the Bible*, edited by Kevin J. VanHoozer, 559–62. Grand Rapids: Baker, 2005.

Yadin, Yigael. "The Mystery of the Unexplained Chains: A Chain Reaction at Lachish." *BAR* 10 (1984) 65–67.

Yamauchi, Edwin M. *Foes from the Northern Frontiers: Invading Hordes from the Russian Steppes.* 1982, Reprint, Eugene, OR: Wipf & Stock, 2003.

Zimmerli, Walter. *Ezekiel 1: A Commentary on the Book of the Prophet Ezekiel, Chapters 1–24.* Translated by Ronald E. Clements. Edited by Frank Moore Cross and Klaus Baltzer, with Leonard Jay Greenspoon. Hermeneia. Philadelphia: Fortress, 1979.

Index of Ancient Documents

2 Chronicles

Ezra

Nehemiah

Job

Psalms

Proverbs

Isaiah

Isaiah *(continued)*

Jeremiah

Ezekiel *(continued)*

Revelation *(continued)*

EARLY CHRISTIAN WRITINGS

Eusebius

Church History